T0294622

Commemoration

About the Series

The American Association for State and Local History Book Series addresses issues critical to the field of state and local history through interpretive, intellectual, scholarly, and educational texts. To submit a proposal or manuscript to the series, please request proposal guidelines from AASLH headquarters: AASLH Editorial Board, 2021 21st Ave. South, Suite 320, Nashville, Tennessee 37212. Telephone: (615) 320–3203. Website: www.aaslh.org.

About the Organization

The American Association for State and Local History (AASLH) is a national history membership association headquartered in Nashville, Tennessee. AASLH provides leadership and support for its members who preserve and interpret state and local history in order to make the past more meaningful to all Americans. AASLH members are leaders in preserving, researching, and interpreting traces of the American past to connect the people, thoughts, and events of yesterday with the creative memories and abiding concerns of people, communities, and our nation today. In addition to sponsorship of this book series, AASLH publishes *History News* magazine, a newsletter, technical leaflets and reports, and other materials; confers prizes and awards in recognition of outstanding achievement in the field; supports a broad education program and other activities designed to help members work more effectively; and advocates on behalf of the discipline of history. To join AASLH, go to www.aaslh.org or contact Membership Services, AASLH, 2021 21st Ave. South, Suite 320, Nashville, TN 37212.

Commemoration

The American Association for State and Local History Guide

Edited by Seth C. Bruggeman

ROWMAN & LITTLEFIELD
Lanham · Boulder · New York · London

Published by Rowman & Littlefield
A wholly owned subsidary of The Rowman & Littlefield Publishing Group, Inc.
4501 Forbes Boulevard, Suite 200, Lanham, Maryland 20706
www.rowman.com

Unit A, Whitacre Mews, 26–34 Stannary Street, London SE11 4AB

British Library Cataloguing-in-Publication Information Available

Library of Congress Cataloging-in-Publication Data

Names: Bruggeman, Seth C., 1975– editor. | American Association for State and Local History.
Title: Commemoration : the American Association for State and Local History guide / edited by Seth C. Bruggeman.
Description: Lanham, Maryland : Rowman & Littlefield Publishing Group, 2017. | Includes bibliographical references and index.
Identifiers: LCCN 2017032556 (print) | LCCN 2017033231 (ebook) | ISBN 9781442279209 (Electronic) | ISBN 9781442279186 (cloth : alk. paper) | ISBN 9781442279193 (pbk. : alk. paper)
Subjects: LCSH: Memorialization—United States. | Memorials—United States. | Collective memory—United States. | United States—Anniversaries, etc. | United States—History, Local—Anniversaries, etc. | Anniversaries—United States. | Public history—United States.
Classification: LCC E179 (ebook) | LCC E179 .C655 2017 (print) | DDC 973—dc23
LC record available at https://lccn.loc.gov/2017032556

♾™ The paper used in this publication meets the minimum requirements of American National Standard for Information Sciences—Permanence of Paper for Printed Library Materials, ANSI/NISO Z39.48–1992.

Printed in the United States of America

Contents

List of Illustrations

FIGURES

Acknowledgments

This book, and my role in crafting it, owe considerably to early encouragement from John Dichtl and Bob Beatty. Bob provided sound guidance throughout and even agreed to be a contributor despite his many other commitments. The editorial team—Charles Harmon, Kathleen E. O'Brien, Melissa McNitt, and Brindha Thirumoorthy—moved through the stages of production at lighting speed. Andrew Lopez prepared a fine index; Rebecca Shrum eased some late-stage anxieties; and Hilary Iris Lowe worked her usual magic in all matters of love and writing. Juniata Gladys Bruggeman makes paper airplanes and laughs all the while.

I owe special thanks to this volume's contributors, all of whom I hold in the highest regard. Their work, and the AASLH's support of it, reminds us that doing history is a social act in which we all have a stake.

Figure 1.1.   Russell Lee, *Bicycle riders in parade on the Fourth of July at Vale, Oregon.* July, 1941. Library of Congress

Chapter 1

Introduction

Conundrum and Nuance in American Memory

Seth C. Bruggeman

Commemoration is the lingua franca of public memory. It encompasses all the various ways people have imagined—in monuments, ceremonies, festivals, pageants, fairs, museums, reenactment, and more—to conjure deep regard for the past. Unlike history, which is concerned primarily with circumstance, commemoration dwells almost entirely in feeling. It is for this reason that we all recognize commemoration, and understand it for the most part, even when it doesn't speak directly to us. But how should we manage it? On first take, it seems that planning historical anniversaries or reenactments might not be any different than staging any of the myriad other programs that sustain our nation's heritage landscape. Consider, though, the cultural work that commemoration does, and the picture becomes less clear. The incredible diversity of rituals, objects, and customs that we associate with commemoration is all intended to give public feeling to otherwise-private memories. The problem, of course, is that there are as many ways to remember as there are people with memories. So what is the best way to make memory public? And what happens when we share our memories, including with those who feel differently about them than we do?[1]

These are just a few of the questions that this volume seeks to answer. It certainly won't be the first to try. Rather, a whole industry of memory studies has grown up around the study of commemoration. Much of this scholarship reflects a growing concern, particularly during the past three decades, with the production and maintenance of nationalism. Drawing on the pioneering works of Benedict Anderson, Pierre Nora, and others, memory scholars have made remarkable strides toward identifying how heritage landscapes everywhere make and break national bonds, particularly in times of patriotic distress. We discover, for instance, that in the United States, some of the most enduring sites of pubic memory—examples include George Washington's

Mount Vernon, Independence Hall, the Vietnam Veterans Memorial Wall—
were most vigorously enshrined during turbulent postwar years. We discover
too that all of these places, iconic though they may be, have prompted considerable debate over the meaning of citizenship and the promise of American
democracy.[2]

As fruitful as this scholarship has been, its rewards have been less forthcoming to heritage professionals for whom sifting through stacks of books
is a practical impossibility. What's more, the theoretical contexts that make
memory studies so rich also tend to obscure key findings for readers who
aren't accustomed to the perplexities of scholarly writing. Even those who are
will discover very little in this body of work pertaining to the practicalities of
commemoration. How does one, after all, mount a commemorative event that
accommodates diverse stakeholders who remember differently? Is it possible
to align the practical demands of fund-raising and facilities management with
a commemorative practice that avoids ideological entanglements? If so, how?

Commemoration makes the findings of memory studies more readily accessible by serving as a provocation for site mangers, heritage professionals, and
all manner of public historians who contend daily with the ground-level com-
plexities of commemoration. Our chapters are intended as tools insomuch as
each provides insight for practitioners, and the boards and foundations that
fund them, confronted with common problems in commemorative practice
today. Our concern here has not been to dwell at length on matters of definition or to revisit well-trodden paths through the evolution of commemorative
practice, but rather to glimpse commemoration as it is practiced now within
the historical contexts that give it meaning and with an eye to the challenges
it faces going forward. Nor have we sought to be encyclopedic. Our focus
is delineated in large part by who we are, an ad hoc affiliation of heritage
professionals and fellow travelers. Although commemoration happens in all
aspects of life, our perspective in this volume is largely institutional because
it reflects the particularities of our professional concerns. Our goal is to help
others, especially those working amid a host of dire economic and political
threats to cultural nonprofit organizations, stage thoughtful commemorative
events that have significant impact across a range of audiences.

THE COMMEMORATIVE CONUNDRUM OVER TIME

By virtue of its immediacy, and in view of its authorship, this volume is its
own kind of commemorative endeavor. Readers will find enshrined here
a monument to the commemorative ethos that prevails among American
(mostly) heritage professionals witness to the turn of the twenty-first century.
It is a distinctly different vision than what Robert G. Hartje imagined in the

AASLH's last guide to commemoration: *Bicentennial USA: Pathways to Celebration* (1973). Hartje's task in that volume was to prepare local, state, and regional planners to manage celebrations surrounding the 200th anniversary of the birth of the United States. The bicentennial was—as he put it "a once-in-a-lifetime affair, a chance to step outside the routines of daily living and look at the past—to evaluate, appreciate, and preserve that which gives the nation and its people identify."[3] Our purpose, more than four decades after Hartje, is hardly so singular. And our outlook is distinguished by a prevailing notion that commemoration's power unfolds within daily lives, not beyond them.

Our vision is very much like Hartje's, however, insomuch as it is "complicated by the current mood in America and the world." For Hartje and his readers, the complexity owed to a core concern: American democracy, in its 200th year, seemed everywhere in peril. Economic uncertainty, raging inequality, and violence at home and abroad dominated headlines in the years leading to the bicentennial. Some citizens, Hartje warned, "may not want to involve themselves in commemoration of a period so remote and alien to their present mode of life."[4] Today's headlines are not so different. Nor it seems are the commemorative anxieties that await any honest reckoning with the past. Even forty years since Hartje warned us against repeating the missteps of the 1961–1965 Civil War Centennial, for instance, which "rekindled old flames that still smoldered as embers," we still need reminded—as Rick Beard, Bob Beatty, and George McDaniel do in this volume—that those embers burn on.[5]

How is it that we seem constantly to forget this lesson? And why is it that we can't ever seem to disentangle commemoration from politics? In part, the answer lies within commemoration's central conundrum: for everything remembered, something gets forgotten. It's an insight that wasn't readily evident to Hartje and others who understood commemoration as dictionaries still define it today, "a calling to remembrance, or preserving in memory, by some solemn observance, public celebration, etc."[6] A generation of memory scholarship has encouraged us to embrace a rather more capacious notion of what commemoration is and how it works. Foremost among its lessons is the extent to which memories, as John Gillis puts it, "are not things we think *about*, but things we think *with*."[7] Public memory, in other words, is carefully constructed over time by people who make purposeful decisions about what to remember and what not to. Commemoration finesses all of the decisions, and all of the arguments that preceded them, into a singular vision of the past that delivers one message with one voice to all audiences. When we visit a monument, therefore, we remember the war or person or event, but not necessarily the arguments about how it might be otherwise remembered. Commemoration is an argument about the past presented as if there were no argument.

It is this facet of commemoration, its promise of a reprieve from argument, which explains in part why we find it so alluring, and why we so readily forget its risks. Site managers especially whose livelihoods depend on welcoming visitors have good reason to fear argument. And who can quibble with the commemorative impulse to celebrate people and events for whom considerable good will seems everywhere evident? In this volume, Jean-Pierre Morin does just that by showing us how our notions about who deserves to be commemorated—Canada's "great men" in his chapter—have also been constructed for us over time, in this instance by politicians eager to consolidate power. It is an important point, famously made by Kirk Savage who years ago demonstrated how virtually every Civil War monument constructed during the turn of the last century, no matter where or by whom it was built, argued silently for the perpetuation of an American racial hierarchy. In fact, the same ideas about manhood, social class, and heritage communicated through that era's commemorative landscape appear to persist in our own era's preoccupation with battle reenactment. As Cathy Stanton shows us, Civil War reenactors especially bring to their craft a whole host of anxieties born of the past and filtered through their experience of postindustrial America. In each of these examples, we see that commemoration, no matter how vigorously it nods toward consensus, is never free of argument.

When memory scholars refer to the politics of commemoration, this is precisely what they are talking about: the tendency of commemoration to obscure decisions made about who gets remembered and why. Indeed, our habits of memory have a history of their own that predisposes them to erasure. Returning to Hartje, for instance, we might consider the nation's first commemorative enterprise: remembering the Revolution. Commemoration in that case began even before the war ended. Memorial sermons and battlefield tours in Lexington and Concord, blockbuster fourth-of-July celebrations in Philadelphia, and even the careful editing of George Washington's wartime papers by his assistants at Mount Vernon—all sought to remember for the world a war won decisively by virtuous men in defense of liberty.[8] But because the founding generation presumed that virtue inheres primarily in white landholding men, the memories it produced deviated from reality in significant ways. Most famous, perhaps, is Paul Revere's 1770 portrayal of the Boston Massacre wherein blood-thirsty British troops fire into a gathering of white American gentlemen. The reality, of course, was much different. Historians have written volumes about the racially diverse working people who actually came to blows with beleaguered British troops on that most remembered of days. Crispus Attucks, recalled as the Massacre's (and perhaps the war's) first victim, became a mixed-race *cause célèbre* among abolitionists and is still celebrated today, especially in Boston, in festivals and memorials. Despite all of this, however, Revere's propaganda, a clever gambit to generate support for the war, has endured as commemorative truth for nearly two and a half centuries.[9]

From the outset, then, our eagerness to nourish American ambition has made a degree of amnesia seem perfectly acceptable in our commemorative work. Consequently, our earliest memories of the Revolution "forgot" the array of difference that typified life in early America. They also led us to believe that the patriotic unity we aspire to today somehow echoes conditions on the ground during the 1780s. This too is a fiction. In fact, commemoration after the war slowed down precipitously because nobody was entirely sure what, if anything, all the fighting had accomplished. The government it created under the Articles of Confederation succumbed in less than a decade to the radically different vision of a few elite statesmen. And clearly, given the persistence of inequality along lines of race, class, and gender, the ideals of liberty set forth by the founding generation had very obvious limitations. Historian Michael A. McDonnell notes that, to move past the Revolution's problematic legacy and to build a functional nationalism, Americans set out after the war to forget its most troubling contradictions. But "forgetting," as he puts it, "was a political project and it took time."[10]

In fact, it took about a half century. Beyond a smattering of early tributes to the war, such as Charles Bulfinch's 1789 monument atop Boston's Beacon Hill, Americans reserved their commemorative energies primarily for George Washington, for whom monuments appeared high above Baltimore and deep within rural Virginia by 1815. By 1817, Washington devotees could enjoy a veritable theme park of revolutionary memorabilia and costumed performance at his adopted grandson's new Arlington House.[11] Arlington reflected the extent to which Revolutionary memory weighed heavy on the minds of Americans in the years following the War of 1812. Just as we lament the passing of World War II veterans, vanguards of the so-called greatest generation, Americans during the 1820s valorized the lives of a vanishing generation of Revolutionary war soldiers.[12] The nostalgic national tour of General Lafayette in 1824–1825 reinforced the tendency to think of veterans, including Lafayette himself, as sacred relics of a bygone era.[13] Interestingly, for years after the war, veterans remembered it in decidedly unglamorous terms.[14] Written accounts of the war shifted significantly, however, by the 1820s, and increasingly featured the patriotic tropes that have become so common today.[15]

It was a shift, incidentally, that coincided with the deaths of the Revolution's last living icons: Thomas Jefferson (1826), John Adams (1826), and James Monroe (1831). And it was precisely that generation's unfinished business, ironically, that intensified longing in subsequent decades for its supposed virtue. The political and cultural machinations required to sustain slavery in the young republic introduced tremendous anxiety into the nation's commemorative landscape. As historian Alfred F. Young shows in his account of Boston shoemaker cum revolutionary, George Robert Twelves Hewes, much of our memory of the Revolution was concocted during the 1830s by anxious politicians in their campaign against abolitionists and others who struggled to make real the promises of American liberty. As Young puts it, the actual legacy of workaday men like Hewes "was taken over by such conservatives [who] tamed him, sanitizing him and the audacious popular movement he had been a part of."[16] Even the Bunker Hill monument's 1843 dedication ceremony sparked outrage among abolitionists when it appeared—wrongly, it turns out—that President John Tyler, invited to speak at the dedicatory ceremonies, brought along an enslaved man to hold his parasol.[17] These examples illustrate that because the Revolution's legacy was so ambiguous, its memory could be populated with no end of contradictory meanings, and by people on either extreme of the political spectrum.

It was the powerful interweaving of abolitionist sentiment and Revolutionary memory in fact that inspired what has since become one of the most persistently influential visions of our nation's founding saga. Henry Wadsworth Longfellow's *Paul Revere's Ride* (1861) has long passed as a staple of patriotic Americana, a poem to be memorized by school children and presidents.[18] It made a national hero of Revere whose notoriety had previously been limited to New England.[19] And, for generations of readers, it transformed the Revolution from a vague concept into a palpable event wherein real places—the Old North Church, Boston harbor, Charlestown, and all "the roofs of the town"—carried the action. What its ubiquity has obscured, however, as scholars and pundits have dwelled on at length, is that Longfellow's most famous poem was mostly fiction, crafted in the moment to raise up northerners against the terrors of chattel slavery.[20] It is a masterstroke of abolitionist writing that relied upon the prevailing imagery of its time, namely nostalgic invocations of the American Revolution, to warn of a lurking evil that threatened to destroy the nation if not defeated. Most of us, then, when we recall Paul Revere's bravery, aren't recalling the Revolution so much as the revolutionary intensity of the struggle against slavery.

The Revolution is certainly not the only event that has been remembered and reremembered for us over the generations by people with competing political interests. Most obviously, and perhaps most publicly, the Civil War has consumed American commemorative preoccupations since its start. My point, however, in exploring the particularities of Revolutionary memory is to highlight three lessons that bear on all commemorative work no matter its topic or intent. First, and as we've seen vividly in the case of the Revolution, commemoration is always political because choosing what to remember is a way of exercising power over people and ideas who are left out of our historical imagination. Second, memories have histories of their own. Interrogating the history of our commemorative impulses often reveals that the way we remember today—no matter how original it may seem—perpetuates ideas and values from the past that may or may not nourish our hopes for the future. Third, and finally, memory has inertia. A memory put in motion tends to stay in motion. Commemoration has the power to accelerate certain memories while diverting others. If history is any indicator, then the people we rely on to make these decisions, and the ways in which they do it, bear considerable weight on our nation's destiny.

A PATH TO NUANCE

Inaccessibility notwithstanding, it may be that another reason why memory scholarship hasn't had a fuller impact on commemorative practice is because its findings are, well, depressing. Time and time again, as with the Revolution, we discover that our heroes were not so heroic or that our reasons for honoring them were not as pure as we'd like to believe. Here and there we discover stories about people who, though otherwise disregarded by time, manage to assert their voices through purposeful acts of commemoration. Their victories, however, appear fleeting and more often we learn that commemoration, though run through with democratic appeals, reflects rather the interests of the wealthy, the powerful, and the normative. In these accounts, the people tasked with staging commemoration—those belonging, that is, to monument commissions, historical associations, civic organizations, museum staffs, and other progenitors of today's heritage professions—typically end up being complicit in or victims of all sorts of unsavory politics and moneymaking schemes. Consider in chapter 5, for instance, Anne C. Reilly's portrayal of early twentieth-century Plymoutheans who, despite their best intentions, lost control of Plymouth Rock's commemorative meanings amid a flurry of competing interests. The problem is not that these accounts aren't true—they most certainly are—but rather that they convey a bleak inevitability. Is it even possible for us to manage commemoration in a way that avoids the pitfalls of the past?

Our hope in this volume is to suggest that, not only is it possible, but that doing commemoration and getting it right may be more important than ever before. Certainly, all of our readers understand that the acute political partisanship of our time has undermined traditional sources of public support, both intellectual and financial, for arts and cultural programing in the United States. But what may be even more corrosive, for our purposes, are the habits of mind that have emerged amid the denigration of public culture. The late proliferation of so-called fake news, for instance, reveals a broad demographic of Americans that is either unable or unwilling to acknowledge that headlines—not unlike memories—are contrived by people whose intentions are not reliably virtuous. Paired with the crisis of discernment is the predominance of affect—especially grief, fear, gratitude, shame, and anger, as Erika Doss figures it—throughout public culture, and especially in the memorials that pop up everywhere it seems these days.[21] Emotion is a cornerstone of commemoration because of its uncanny ability to reveal commonalities among uncommon people. And yet equally uncanny is its tendency to obscure the complexity of the people and events we recall. Mourning alone, for instance, does not explain how a wrongful death could have been avoided, or who should be held accountable for it. The Internet, of course, has exacerbated the worst of these tendencies even while it has democratized commemoration in ways that Hartje and his generation could never have imagined.

What is missing, and what the following chapters suggest that commemoration can and should strive for, is precisely what social media, roadside memorials, and the 24/7 news cycle abhor: nuance. Like argument, nuance and its predilection for shades of meaning may not seem like a winning strategy for door sales, but then again our audiences are changing it seems as quickly as our political landscape. Patrick Grossi who, in chapter 11, perceives powerful synergies between commemoration and social activism, suggests that nuance and emotion are hardly incompatible. On the contrary, together they encourage "recognition of people's shared and unique experiences." Commemoration that appreciates the simultaneity of shared and individual experience, Grossi points out, demonstrates relevance to "its intended audience," even while challenging "the assumptions of audiences further afield." It's a lesson, in fact, we might take from Doss's observations on the rise of affect. Our need to feel with others is, in essence, a desire to recognize our individuality within a greater whole. In this light, commemoration, which has for so long sought as Hartje did to appreciate "that which gives the nation and its people identify," might rather seek to appreciate how individuals go about defining and redefining the nation over time. It is individuals, after all, as Tammy Gordon concludes in our introductory chapter, that "do the work of creating meaning from the passage of time, events, and people."

Decentering the very of concept of nation is another strategy explored here for encouraging commemorative nuance. Commemoration that begins from a desire to celebrate the nation often presumes that everyone understands "nation" in the same terms. Nothing could be farther from the truth. Is the United States a place? Maybe it's a sequence of places? Or is it a concept? A set of laws? Manifest opportunity, or maybe the opposite? Maybe it's all of this, or none of it? Everyone has a different answer. In fact, as William A. Walker shows us in chapter 3, commemorative festivals flourish when Americans are most conflicted about the meaning of nation. Ethnic festivals, especially, have served over time either to argue for a more expansive definition of America or to limit its terms to a select few. Decentering nation, then, not only encourages nuance but also expands commemoration's audience to include Americans for whom citizenship is neither simple nor assured. This is not to say, however, that we ought to exclude nation from our commemorative framework. On the contrary, as Adam Hjorthén argues in chapter 7, understanding that all of our communities are in one way or the other run through with global connections creates opportunities to appreciate the fascinating interplay of national identities over time. For savvy planners, it also creates opportunities for cost sharing and the delegation of commemorative labors across national borders.

All of this, from teasing out individual experience to revealing global interconnectedness, is complicated work, and its success depends on vigorous collaboration. Collaboration and creative partnership building verge on cliché in modern heritage discourse, and so it is important to be clear about terms. For much of its history, commemorative practice revolved around the decisions of a select group of people—a monument commission, for instance—charged with delivering ideas about our past to the public. The chapters in this volume endorse a very different approach wherein commemorative planning begins and ends in conversation with the many publics it might potentially serve. The result, detailed, for instance, in Devin C. Manzullo-Thomas's fascinating reflection in chapter 10 on the interplay of religion and commemoration, is not just a more meaningful commemoration but an opportunity to encourage conversation among people otherwise distanced by matters as profound as faith. Paying for commemoration also requires creative partnership building, especially for planners keen to avoid the ideological entanglements of private funding. Janet L. Gallimore shows us how to do it in chapter 6 by recalling her work with everyone from Idaho's first lady to its state lottery commission. Finally, if nuance is our goal, then commemorative partnerships must always include trained historians who understand the people and events being commemorated as well as the times and places they are being commemorated in. As we see throughout this volume, the historian's voice is an essential bulwark against commemoration's vulnerability to dogma.

Finally, nuanced commemoration must always aspire to transparency and reflexivity. The notion that commemoration reveals more about us than the people and events that we remember has become gospel in memory scholarship, and for good reason.[22] Commemoration is a mirror. Reflected in portrayals of the past are glimpses of today's hopes, fears, insecurities, and grudges. All of this is evident to those who don't share our commemorative outlook and, therefore, toward ensuring that celebration doesn't encourage alienation, we must, as Tammy Gordon puts it, be "absolutely transparent and explicit about [our] interpretive approaches." We must, as it were, look in the mirror and be frank about what we see. We must also make clear to our partners that the commemorative work we do today is no longer engaged in the politics of erasure that prevailed for so many generations. An important first step in this direction is documenting ourselves. As Bob Beatty and Rick Beard note in chapter 12, the state of Connecticut's "laudable effort" to document its own Civil War sesquicentennial programming is vitally important "in this age of ephemeral digital communication." Remembering how we remember, then, is as important for establishing accountability in our own time as it is for sharing our legacy with the future.

What's at stake, then, for getting commemoration right? How we answer that question is also a mirror of our times. When work began on this volume, my sense was that the great prize for careful commemoration was the opportunity for individuals and communities to celebrate their own notions of historical commonality, rather than bow to the historical imaginings of profiteers and politicians. Since then, however, my sense is that the stakes have changed. The dramatic reversals on view everywhere now in our political landscape convince me that nuance is more dearly threatened than I had realized. Will its last stand be among the nation's commemorative infrastructure, among the monuments and memorials and festivals wherein for over two centuries, we've argued over the possibilities of American democracy? If so, then it will fall to our readers, a vast network of heritage professionals, to make hard decisions about what it means to remember in modern America. The path forward will not be easy in any case, and so it is our hope that this volume will provide guidance and perhaps a sense of the strength we can find in common cause.

NOTES

1. I owe my understanding of public feeling to Erika Doss, *Memorial Mania: Public Feeling in America* (Chicago, IL; and London: The University of Chicago Press, 2010).

2. The best overview of foundational memory scholarship for heritage professionals remains David Glassberg, "Public History and the Study of Memory," *The Public Historian* 18 (Spring 1996), 7–23.

3. Robert G. Hartje, *Bicentennial USA: Pathways to Celebration* (Nashville, TN: The American Association for State and Local History, 1973), 10.

4. Hartje, *Bicentennial USA*, 15.

5. See, for instance, Modupe Ladobe, "Reconsideration of Memorials and Monuments," *History News* 71:4 (Autumn 2016), 7–11.

6. "Commemoration, n." OED Online. March 2016. Oxford University Press. http://www.oed.com.libproxy.temple.edu/view/Entry/36998, accessed May 31, 2016.

7. John R. Gillis, *Commemorations: The Politics of National Identity* (Princeton, NJ: Princeton University Press, 1994), 5.

8. Scholarly accounts of these instances are prevalent. See, for instance, Bob Gross, "Commemorating Concord," *Common-Place* 4:1 (October 2003), http://www. common-place-archives.org/vol-04/no-01/gross/index.shtml; David Waldstreicher, *In the Midst of Perpetual Fetes: The Making of American Nationalism, 1776–1820* (Chapel Hill: University of North Carolina Press, 1997), especially chapter 1; and Joseph Ellis, *His Excellency: George Washington* (New York: Vintage, 2004), 150.

9. On Crispus Attucks, for instance, see Mitch Kachun, *First Martyr of Liberty: Crispus Attucks in American Memory* (New York: Oxford University Press, 2017).

10. Michael A. McDonnell, "War and Nationhood: Founding Myths and Historical Realities," in McDonnell et al., eds. *Remembering the Revolution: Memory, History, and Nation Making from Independence to the Civil War* (Amherst and Boston: University of Massachusetts press, 2013), 21, 34.

11. On early commemorative architecture associated with George Washington, see Seth C. Bruggeman, *"Here, George Washington was Born": Memory, Material Culture, and the Public History of a National Monument* (Athens: University of Georgia Press, 2008), chapter 1. Custis is profiled in Seth C. Bruggeman, "More than Ordinary Patriotism: Living History in the Memory Work of George Washington Parke Custis," in McDonnell et al., eds. *Remembering the Revolution,* 127–43.

12. Edward Tang, "Writing the American Revolution: War Veterans in the Nineteenth-Century Cultural Memory," *Journal of American Studies* 32:1 (1998), 63–80.

13. See, for instance, Ketih Beutler, "Emma Willard's 'True Mnemonic of History': America's First Textbooks, Proto-Feminism, and the Memory of the Revolution," in McDonnell et al., *Remembering the Revolution,* 169. A great deal has been written about Lafayette and nineteenth-century reliquary sensibilities. See, for instance, Thomas A. Chambers, *Memories of War: Visiting Battlegrounds and Bonefields in the Early American Republic* (Ithaca, NY: Cornell University Press, 2012), chapter 3.

14. On these counts, see William Hunting Howell, "'Starving Memory': Antinarrating the American Revolution," and Caroline Cox, "The First Greatest Generation Remembers the Revolutionary War," both in McDonnell et al., *Remembering the Revolution.*

15. McDonnell et al., "The Revolution in American Life from 1776 to the Civil War," in McDonnell et al., eds. *Remembering the Revolution,* 2.

16. See Alfred F. Young, *The Shoemaker and the Tea Party: Memory and the American Revolution* (Boston, MA: Beacon Press, 2000). The quote is from Young, "Revolution in Boston? Eight Propositions for Public History on the Freedom Trail," *The Public Historian* 25 (Spring 2003), 30.

17. Although Tyler was not, in fact, accompanied on stage by a slave, Boston's abolitionist press leveraged the nonincident in its indictment of the federal government's complicity in the national crime of slavery. Margot Minardi, *Making Slavery History: Abolitionism and the Politics of Memory in Massachusetts* (New York: Oxford University Press, 2010), 83–89.

18. Robert Pinsky observed that Senator Edward Kennedy had memorized portions of the poem. See Robert Pinsky, "Poetry and American memory," *The Atlantic* (October 1999), 60.

19. Revere had earned some notoriety in Boston by the middle of the nineteenth century but barely figured at all in Americans' memory of the Revolution. David Hacket Fischer, *Paul Revere's Ride* (New York and Oxford: Oxford University Press, 1994), 331.

20. Several scholars have explored the poem's long-unrecognized abolitionist intent, including Jill Lepore, "How Longfellow Woke the Dead," *The American Scholar* (Spring 2011). Lepore further considers the role of Revolutionary Memory in recent politics in *The Whites of Their Eyes: The Tea Party's Revolution and the Battle over American History* (Princeton and Oxford: Princeton University Press, 2010). Also see Kammen, *A Season of Youth*, chapter 4; and, Evert Jan van Leeuwen, "The Graveyard Aesthetics of Revolutionary Elegiac Verse: Remembering the Revolution as a Sacred Cause," in McDonnell et al., *Remembering the Revolution*, 75–76.

21. Doss, *Memorial Mania* is organized around these five emotions.

22. See, for instance, Dell Upton, "Why Do Contemporary Monuments Talk So Much?" in David Gobel and Daves Rossell, eds. *Commemoration in America: Essays on Monuments, Memorialization, and Memory* (Charlottesville and London: University of Virginia Press, 2013), 11–35.

Figure 2.1.   Prince memorial, April 2017, Minnesota History Center. Courtesy of the MNHS.

Chapter 2

The Exhibition and the Funeral

Commemoration as Display

Tammy S. Gordon

We begin at the end, as it were, with Tammy Gordon's astute observation that "exhibitions are the funerals for history." If we are, as she puts it, "the funeral directors for our own history," then how exactly should we relate to the deceased? And what are our responsibilities to the bereaved? Although this is just the first of several essays concerning various modes of commemoration, it introduces themes that will reappear throughout our volume. We learn, for instance, about the importance of collaborative planning. We see too how the wages of violence, and public demand for catharsis, are reshaping the curatorial voice in our own time. And we are reminded that though new technologies reach larger audiences than ever before, and in more places than we might expect, individuals still stand at the center of all commemorative enterprise.

—ed.

Consider for a moment—and bear with me on this, dear reader—how exhibitions and funerals function similarly in American society. With a number of significant differences defined by culture and geography, most funerals in the United States will offer some sort of display: the display of a deceased body (either in a quasi-taxidermied state in repose with full makeup, or held as ashes and bits in a ceremonial container), the display of mementoes like photos, items belonging to or representing the deceased, or the arrangement of the visual-tactile evidence of the community's mourning in the form of flowers or other items sent to the family by sympathizers. Like funerals, exhibitions mark the passage of time by displaying relics of an era, an event, or a process that had an effect on our lives but is no longer in a familiar, material form. In some ways, but especially in commemoration efforts, exhibitions are the funerals for history. The living pass by the relics of the dead, and celebrate what was, recognize the past's effect on the present, or breathe a sigh of relief that what is gone is really gone. Sometimes an individual visitor/mourner will do all these at once, as he or she is not mutually exclusive.

But have you ever been to a funeral that did not go well? One that brought up unresolved issues and led to confrontation and bad feeling? (If you haven't been to one like this, then maybe you haven't been to enough funerals). What made that funeral less than satisfying for its participants? Did its organizers fail to read the needs of the mourners? Did they arrange something wrong, or say the wrong thing, or fail to include others in the planning? Did someone say something about the deceased that was too accurate for those present to hear, or not accurate enough? A commemorative exhibit, like a funeral, can be satisfying or not, but the emotion of both mean heightened intensity. As the funeral directors for our own history, we curators have to recognize the sociocultural intensity of commemorating the passage of time and at the same time recognize that we cannot use a commemoration to force the resolution of the unresolved. While the dead might be dead, the effects of their actions live. To put the point in its most clichéd form, funerals are for the living.

Even when it's not asked to commemorate, the historical exhibition is one of our most beleaguered media. We expect our exhibits to allow for education, recreation, social interaction, and economic change. As curators, we want our work to respond to the social, physical, cultural, and economic needs of our communities. We expect a lot from a room full of artifacts, graphics, and inter-actives. During times of heightened commemoration, however, exhibits become even more charged with meaning. Two famous examples from the early 1990s illustrate this: "The Last Act: The Atomic Bomb and the End of World War II," an interpretive plan that never materialized as an exhibit; and *First Encounters*, an exhibit marking the quincentenary of the first Columbus voyage.

The interpretive plan for "The Last Act," about which much has been written, has become a culture war veteran's tale on a number of issues from stake-holder involvement to assessment of the political environment.[1] Curators at the Smithsonian National Air and Space Museum planned "The Last Act" as an effort in historical education, not as commemoration. Veterans groups and politicians on the right saw the planned exhibit as ill-suited to the commemo-rative, supposedly patriotic moment of the end of World War II and protested "The Last Act" as a "politically correct" attempt at sullying the reputations of veterans.[2] In the history of exhibition and commemoration, *First Encounters* and the protest surrounding it stand out as a significant moment even though comparatively little has been written about it. Timed to coincide with the Columbus Quincentenary in 1992, curators planned the exhibit without work-ing with American Indian people, and the results were predictable: an exhibit that privileged the European context and protestors who objected to the lack of Indigenous perspective. Protestors used the opportunity of the exhibit as a theatre in which to stage their views.[3]

First Encounters continued to meet protest in its travels, and interpretation remained unaltered from the original until it landed at the Science Museum of Minnesota, which mounted a response exhibit titled *From the Heart of Turtle Island: Native Views* (1992) and included interpretive text in *First Encounters* that encouraged visitors to interrogate the curatorial voice. When American Indian Movement activist Vernon Bellecourt tossed his own blood at a reproduction sail, the museum decided to leave it as representative of views not expressed effectively in the exhibit itself.[4] "The Last Act" interpretive plan and *First Encounters*, while very different curatorial projects for sure, both ended up teaching lessons about the contemporary exhibition's role in public dialogue. For the protestors of *First Encounters*, the commemoration was a moment to mourn; for those who objected to "The Last Act," commemoration was a moment to celebrate. In both cases, curators did not respond quickly enough to their concerns. In other words, they showed up at the funeral to say the thing about the dead that didn't correlate well with the experiences of the living.

In his massive study of memory in modern Chile, Steve J. Stern uses Pierre Nora's idea of the "memory knot" as an important framework for understanding commemoration. He writes that "we can trace the making of influential memory frameworks and sensibilities by focusing on 'memory knots' in society, time, and place. Strongly motivated human groups, symbolically powerful events and anniversary commemoration dates, haunting remains and places—these galvanize struggles to shape and project onto the public cultural domain ways of remembering that capture an essential truth."[5] Pair the memory knot as a highly charged emotional moment with the exhibition from which we as a society expect so much, and the process of curating commemoration becomes, to say the least, difficult.

Since the early 1990s, we've learned a great deal about the power of the exhibition medium, and our focus has shifted tellingly from objects and narrative to visitor meaning-making. Part of this shift has been cultural, as the explosion of the digital world has increasingly raised our expectations for the responsiveness, adaptability, and shareability of the resources of cultural institutions. Nina Simon calls the current wave of engagement "participatory," noting that "in participatory projects, the institution supports multidirectional content experiences."[6] In other words, exhibits are no longer just developed for people, but with people. Museums have become increasingly responsive to public needs, such as the Minnesota Historical Society's opening a display of Prince artifacts within days after the singer's death.[7]

This responsiveness has had its limits, however, as the conversations around #museumsrespondtoferguson have demonstrated. In late 2014, a consortium of museum professionals and writers decried the lack of museum responses to the crises in Ferguson, Missouri, brought on by police officer

Darren Wilson's shooting of Michael Brown, an African American teenager. The consortium asked museums to look within as well as without for ways to address the inequalities present in all communities.[8] By mid-2015, some curators had responded directly to Ferguson with exhibitions. The Newseum had collected items relating to news coverage of Ferguson and displayed them starting in late December of 2014. The Schomburg Center at the New York Public Library and the National Center for Suburban Studies at Hofstra University opened the James Levy-curated exhibit *Black Suburbia: From Levittown to Ferguson* in early October 2015.[9] Digital, crowdsourced curation has allowed for even quicker responses, such as the Maryland Historical Society's *Preserve the Baltimore Uprising 2015 Archive Project*, which allowed for Baltimore residents to share items related to the protest of the death of Freddie Gray; a year later, it had over 2,500 items contributed.[10] With the help of digital technology, events may be instantly commemorated. Unlike the traditional commemorative exhibit, which takes years to produce, the online archive significantly compresses development and production.

Also since the 1990s, we've come to recognize that historical memory, hence commemoration, is transnational, and while the traditional exhibition medium remains fairly fixed in place, its digital counterpart draws IP addresses from varied geopolitical contexts. While commemoration displays may be framed in geopolitical, nationalistic, or even patriotic terms, they find themselves with visitors from other linguistic and national contexts. The Mayrau Mining Museum in the Czech Republic stands as it did on the last working day of the mine, preserved as a display to honor the workers and community that once made it an active place. Its failure in a world economy as a mine is translated to potential in the international tourism market.[11]

The movement of people across borders occurs vastly more often both physically and virtually than it did in the early 1990s. In this period, the rise of the memorial museum has charged the exhibition medium with a less than metaphorical funerary function. In his study of the proliferation of memorial museums across the globe, Paul Williams notes an important departure from traditional history exhibits: voice. While traditional history museums "assemble their exhibitions in more neutral institutional settings, often alongside permanent galleries that showcase less volatile topics," memorial museums see themselves as advocates for victims of human rights abuses.[12] In commemorating, they avoid the international-scientific, "objective" curatorial voice, and they replace it with a voice of unapologetic advocacy. My larger point here is not that all exhibits should take a position of advocacy, but that publicly recognizing the positionality of the curators and the institution could go a long way toward communicating with visitors from increasingly diverse geopolitical contexts.

Exhibitions, because they face so many expectations, need to be absolutely transparent and explicit about their interpretive approaches. When artists display their works, they do so with statements, words recognized as the creator's perspective. Museum exhibits, particularly those formed in response to the memory knot of commemoration, require such an individualized, personalized approach. Institutions don't organize funerals, and they don't attend them. Whether mourning, celebrating, or feeling indifferent, individuals do the work of creating meaning from the passage of time, events, and people.

NOTES

1. See Steven Dubin, *Displays of Power: Controversy in the American Museum from the Enola Gay to Sensation* (New York and London: New York University Press, 1999); Martin Harwitt, *An Exhibit Denied: Lobbying and the History of the Enola Gay* (New York: Copernicus, 1996); Edward T. Linenthal and Tom Engelhardt, *History Wars: The Enola Gay and Other Battles for the American Past* (New York: Holt, 1996). For a more recent and transnational approach, see Lisa Yoneyama, "Battles over Memory in 'Culture Wars': A Trans-Pacific Perspective," *Nanzan Review of American Studies* 32 (2010), 9–20.

2. Mike Wallace, "The Battle of the Enola Gay," in *Mickey Mouse History and Other Essays on American Memory* (Philadelphia, PA: Temple University Press, 1996), 270–318.

3. Karen Coody Cooper, *Spirited Encounters: American Indians Protest Museum Policies and Practices* (Lanham, MD: Alta Mira Press, 2008), 109–113.

4. Cooper, *Spirited Encounters*,115.

5. Steve J. Stern, *Reckoning with Pinochet: The Memory Question in Democratic Chile, 1989–2006* (Durham, NC: Duke University Press, 2010), 10.

6. Nina Simon, *The Participatory Museum* (Santa Cruz, CA: Museum 2.0, 2010), 2.

7. Lori Williamson, "History Is Now: Remembering Prince," http://discussions.mnhs.org/collections/2016/06/history-is-now-remembering-prince-2/ (accessed July 31, 2017).

8. Adrianne Russell, "Joint Statement from Museum Bloggers & Colleagues on Ferguson & Related Events," https://adriannerussell.wordpress.com/2014/12/11/joint-statement-from-museum-bloggers-colleagues-on-ferguson/ (accessed July 31, 2017).

9. Mary Forgione, "Newseum to display items from Ferguson, Mo., coverage of protests," http://www.latimes.com/travel/deals/la-trb-washington-dc-newseum-ferguson-exhibition-20141203-story.html. New York Public Library, (accessed July 31, 2017).

10. Maryland Historical Society, "Home," http://baltimoreuprising2015.org/home (accessed July 31, 2017).

11. Margaret Lindauer, "The Mayrau Mining Museum: Preserving the Past as a Liminal Space in a Liminal Time," in Kendall R. Phillips and G. Mitchell Reyes, eds. *Global Memoryscapes: Contesting Remembrance in a Transnational Age* (Tuscaloosa: The University of Alabama Press, 2011), 94–117.

12. Paul Williams, *Memorial Museums: The Global Rush to Commemorate Atrocities* (Oxford and New York: Berg, 2007), 21.

Figure 3.1.   At the July 3–14, 1974 Festival of American Folklife, Native Americans section, a woman participates in the blanket toss, a game in the World Eskimo Olympics. Smithsonian Institution Archives.

Chapter 3

Festivals as a Commemorative Genre

William S. Walker

Festivals are ubiquitous in the modern commemorative landscape. Music festivals, folk festivals, film festivals, food festivals, holiday festivals, and festival marketplaces too, all imply a convergence of then and now, even if only in gestures to our ancient habit of ritualized celebration. Festivals are especially popular among heritage organizations because, beyond their easy appeals to multiple audiences, they promise at least the possibility of profit. But, as William S. Walker shows us, these simple celebrations of shared pasts have never been just that. Imbued from the outset with a deep sense of religiosity, festivals have served over time to advance especially powerful—though not always overt—arguments about identity, citizenship, and the course of American democracy. Managing these meanings, and being mindful of their impact on the communities we serve, is the special burden awaiting festival planners.

—ed.

Festivals are unstable vehicles for commemoration. Their dynamic and lively nature makes them different from staid ceremonial events. In many commemorative festivals, space exists for the interplay of what the historian John Bodnar called "official" and "vernacular" narratives.[1] Although official entities—state and local governments, booster organizations, museums, and historical societies—often encourage and organize commemorative festivals, participants bring their own ideas and experiences to the festival grounds and construct meaningful perspectives, sometimes in unanticipated ways. Some festivals are more open to this kind of serendipitous meaning making than others, and it is important to distinguish between festivals and pageants, a more tightly controllable form of commemorative activity popular in the late nineteenth and early twentieth centuries. At pageants, official messages often drowned out diverse, vernacular narratives.[2] True festivals, however, involve multiple activities, and usually include some combination of music, dance, and crafts. More important, they offer informal spaces for a variety of participants to engage directly with one another.

Not all festivals are commemorative. Indeed, the primary function of the majority of contemporary festivals is to encourage cultural performance and recognize particular cultural groups as well as trumpet broader conceptions of tradition, pluralism, and multiculturalism. Nevertheless, festival organizers have frequently tied commemorative activities to cultural celebrations, and the history of festivals in the United States is deeply imbricated with the history of race and ethnicity. Festivals have been a critical medium through which ethnocultural groups have navigated the shoals of assimilation, resistance, cultural preservation, and the invention of tradition.[3] Moreover, festivals have been loci of both civic boosterism and ethnic revivalism, and, especially in recent decades, organizers have frequently connected festivals to economic development projects.

The word "festival" is of European origin and refers to a day of feasting, often in honor of a patron saint. In this sense, festivals have served a commemorative function since at least the Middle Ages. More broadly, however, the idea of an event characterized by eating, drinking, music making, dancing, and sharing of material goods—as well as some ritualistic, and often spiritually rooted, activity—is not exclusive to European, or Euro-American cultures. Indeed, it may be a universal human practice, and, undoubtedly, Native, African, and European cultures in North America engaged in both common and particular festive traditions. The Pinkster festival, which was originally a Dutch celebration practiced in New York and New Jersey and which became an important African American holiday in the late eighteenth and early nineteenth centuries, offers a good example of the ways in which festive traditions operated both within cultural groups and cross-culturally in the colonial and early national periods. Market activities, along with games, dancing, music, and drinking, characterized the festival, which lasted for several days. More important, the annual spring holiday provided an opportunity for enslaved Africans and African Americans to reunite with family members, temporarily invert power relations, and gain a measure of limited independence from the surveillance of slave owners.[4]

In the mid- to late-nineteenth century, festivals played a role in the invention of emerging ethnic identities in the United States. In Buffalo, New York in the 1840s and 1850s, for example, "an annual round of public festivals and banquets became the emergent traditions" of Irish Catholic, Scottish, and English New World ethnicities. Later in the century, Eastern European groups coalesced in ethnic associations that celebrated "traditions of the *Vaterland*" through "national parades, festivals, commemorative anniversaries, banquets

with patriotic speeches, and recitations."⁵ In the early- to mid-twentieth century, Scandinavian American groups in the Midwest embraced festivals as
a means of encouraging retention of language and culture, defining ethnic
group boundaries and identities, balancing assimilationism with cultural
particularity, and boosting local economies. This surge of festival creation
paralleled and intersected with the peak period of historical pageantry in the
United States.

Often, festivals were part of larger commemorative events that included
parades, pageants, and political speeches. In Lindsborg, Kansas, in 1912, for
example, Bethany College initiated a Swedish "May Festival" that combined
festival activities, including games, with a parade and pageant.⁶ Similarly,
the 1925 Norse-American Immigrant Centennial at the state fairgrounds in
St. Paul, Minnesota, included music performances, food, arts and crafts, ora-
tions, and religious services and culminated with a *Pageant of the Northmen*,
which drew 15,000 spectators. Pageants were carefully scripted theatrical
performances that narrated the history of a community or group of people.
Mythic traditions and immigrant pioneer ancestors received special attention
in "a dramatic public ritual through which," according to the historian David
Glassberg, "the residents of a town, by acting out the right version of their
past, could bring about some kind of future social and political transformation."⁷ In an increasingly atomizing industrial age, organizers imagined that
historical pageants would encourage community cohesion. Although they
were often connected, festivals and pageants should not be conflated with
one another. Festivals often included ritualized activities, but they were not
scripted, as were dramatic performances. If pageants were organized and
tightly controlled stage plays, festivals were more like improvisation. Organizers may have set the parameters of interaction and created much of the
scene set, but the actors—that is, the participants—made up their own scripts.
Nevertheless, in the 1910s and 1920s, festivals *and* pageants were critical
sites through which first-, second-, and third-generation Americans wrestled
with defining both ethnic and national identity as nativism permeated U.S.
society and culture. Commemorating immigrant ancestors and celebrating
traditions—even if they had only recently been invented—became ways to
mark a benign form of pluralism while asserting a community's essential
middle-class American identity.

The 1930s witnessed a burgeoning interest in folk culture, and festivals
were key sites where traditions both old and new were on display. The
National Folk Festival, founded in 1934 by Sarah Knott, brought the pioneering idea of a multicultural festival of music, dance, and crafts first to St. Louis
and then Washington, D.C., where it relocated in 1938.⁸ This period also
saw the rising popularity of folklorists including John and Alan Lomax, Carl
Sandburg, Zora Neale Hurston, Benjamin Botkin, and others who brought

aspects of vernacular culture to broad audiences. Neither their work nor the National Folk Festival was particularly commemorative; rather, they were driven by what Alan Lomax would later call "cultural equity," the principle that subaltern cultures should not be overwhelmed and homogenized by the juggernaut of mass entertainment.[9] Folklorists and other aficionados of traditional culture had an important role to play in validating, supporting, and disseminating music and other cultural forms that typically did not receive airplay on radio or, later, television. In some sense, folklorists were commemorating ways of life from the past and collecting scraps of tradition before they vanished forever. More central to their cause, however, was the project of locating and honoring "tradition bearers" and constructing what might be called an American folk canon, a body of stories, songs, crafts, and other materials that represented the diversity and richness of vernacular culture in the United States. Carl Sandburg's influential volume *American Songbag* and the Lomaxes' songbooks provided archetypal models. Their inclusive and pluralistic vision would be echoed in folk festivals, including the National Folk Festival and, later, the Newport Folk Festival and the Smithsonian's Festival of American Folklife.

At the same time, festivals that focused on particular ethnic groups continued to be developed and, in some cases, they flourished as never before. In the early 1930s, Holland, Michigan, created an event called "Tulip Time" to honor the city's Dutch heritage. The event started as a horticultural festival but quickly added a "Dutch market, Dutch-language church services, Dutch cultural parades, and regular performances by *klompen* (wooden shoe) dancers traditionally dressed in the most colorful Dutch costumes."[10] The combination was a wild success and, by the mid-1930s, it was attracting over half a million visitors annually. As with similar festivals, "Tulip Time" was characterized by a negotiation between assimilation and cultural retention. Because the city's residents were increasingly removed from their Dutch ancestors, however, the festival presented a hybrid Dutch-American identity, which was more invention and fantasy than an actual reflection of traditional Dutch culture. As a result, according to the historian Michael Douma, "Tulip Time became an unintentional caricature of Dutch culture and an affirmation of how Americanized the Dutch Americans had actually become."[11] Perhaps more important than the negotiation of ethnic identity was the festival's economic role. During the hard years of the Great Depression, "Tulip Time" became "an essential contributor to the city of Holland's financial well-being."[12] Holland's example serves as a harbinger of later trends in heritage tourism through which deindustrializing municipalities imagined cultural events as economic development bonanzas and cure-alls.

Another ethnic festival from the 1930s featured a similar mix of identity negotiation and economic development. In 1934, Los Angeles's "Little

Tokyo" district initiated a Nisei Week Festival the goals of which were to attract patrons—including both whites and Nisei, or second-generation Japanese Americans—to the district's shops and restaurants and showcase Japanese American identity and culture. "By joining Japanese dance, music, and cultural and martial arts exhibits with a parade, beauty pageant, and other American traditions," the historian Lon Kurashige writes, "the festival presented a harmonious blending of East and West."[13] The event highlighted the kimono, which was prominently displayed in fashion shows, and the *ondo* dance, which became a central showpiece. Ultimately, through demonstrations such as these, the Japanese American Citizens League and the festival's organizers were able to present a vision of Japanese American identity that was attractive to whites while still recognizably Japanese. The internment of thousands of Japanese Americans during World War II disrupted the Nisei Week Festival, but it was restarted in 1949 and continues today.[14] Elsewhere, similar ethnic festivals also persisted after the war. Lindsborg, Kansas's Swedish festival, for example, was rechristened under the name "'Svensk Hyllnings Fest' or Swedish Festival of Tribute" in 1941, and, like Nisei Week, it continues to the present.[15]

In the 1960s, two nationally significant folk festivals captured the spirit of the decade. The Newport Folk Festival (1959) and the Smithsonian's Festival of American Folklife (1967) were pluralistic and inclusive, and both combined eclectic performances with variegated craft displays. Although both festivals, which occurred annually during the summer months, lionized traditional cultures and tradition bearers, neither was explicitly commemorative. An exception was the twelve-week-long folklife festival the Smithsonian mounted in 1976 to mark the Bicentennial of the American Revolution.[16] "Bicenfest" was a monumental undertaking that attracted millions of visitors, but it had very little, if anything, to do with the American Revolution. Instead, it was, in the words of the festival's main organizer and driving force, Ralph Rinzler, "a festival to cherish our differences."

Unlike the tall ships, fireworks displays, and patriotic tchotchkes typically associated with the Bicentennial, the folklife festival focused squarely on the diverse cultural traditions of the United States. Its organizers consciously strove to facilitate meaningful interactions among cultural practitioners, visitors, and scholars from a sweeping range of cultural backgrounds. The festival's mix of performances, demonstrations, and discussions provided numerous opportunities for informal exchanges and unexpected encounters among people. In the "Native Americans" section, for example, visitors heard, and had the opportunity to question, tribal representatives who discussed everything from treaty violations and the federal policy of termination to stereotypes and fishing rights. In other sections, including "Regional America," "Old Ways in the New World," "African Diaspora," and "Working

Americans," festival visitors met African American basket makers and story-tellers, Cajun musicians, and Native artists and witnessed many more engaging presentations. An effusive visitor summed up the experience in a letter to the Secretary of the Smithsonian: "For ten weekends during the summer, I had the best time of my whole entire life, and it was all due to the Festival. . . . Each week, I came away with the feeling that I had come to know myself a bit better, the participants a bit better, their country and my country a bit better."[17] In one sense, this statement illuminates how the festival's therapeutic conception of pluralism had succeeded in diverting attention from deep and persistent divisions and inequalities in U.S. society. At the same time, such a statement demonstrates the stunningly effective ways in which the Bicentennial Festival of American Folklife encouraged transformative cross-cultural interactions.

Bicenfest's emphasis on pluralism corresponded with the localized character of many community-based Bicentennial projects. If Americans could not agree on a single, unifying message in the polarized decade of the 1970s, they had no trouble organizing local observances. Under the loose umbrella of the American Revolution Bicentennial Administration, thousands of cultural events took place in the mid-1970s. At the same time, local historical societies flourished and countless historic house museums were founded or revitalized. Commemorating the Bicentennial became a local and variegated process rather than a unified, top-down endeavor.[18]

In addition to the Bicentennial, the decade of the 1970s also witnessed the ethnic revival, which led to the reinvigoration of festive traditions. Italian-American feasts, for example, were critical sites for negotiating one's ethnic and national identities. Tracing their lineage to the saint's days of the Middle Ages and the local traditions of southern Italian villages, these feasts became, in an American context, loci for renewed ethnic pride in a period that saw the rise of identity politics. Driven at least in part by the immense popularity of Alex Haley's *Roots* and the television miniseries it inspired, white Americans fervently embraced genealogy and explorations of their own ethnic roots in these years. For some, this embrace of ethnic identity was a way to respond to the argument emanating from the civil rights and Black Power movements that the dominant power structure benefited all whites at the expense of people of color.[19] Associating oneself with an ethnic group that had experienced discrimination in the past became a way to disavow what a later generation would call "white privilege"—or the idea that no matter one's ancestry, one's white skin color granted privileges in U.S. society, such as access to certain jobs and respectful treatment from police officers. For many, ethnic revivalism was also a means of constructing a meaningful identity and worldview in an alienating socioeconomic environment. Festivals provided a visual manifestation of individuals' search for meaning and community in a modern industrial or post-industrial age. In this sense, these events were not all that different from the ethnic festivals of the nineteenth and early twentieth centuries, balancing ethnic particularism with broader notions of Americanness. Indeed, this balancing act is one of the consistent themes of commemorative festival making from the nineteenth century to the present.

The other persistent theme is economic development and civic boosterism. As cultural tourism and heritage tourism moved to the center of state and local planners' development projects, festivals became critical elements in the response to faltering regional economies. The argument from boosters is that festivals generate revenue while highlighting the distinctive characteristics of a place. This, of course, is not a new prescription for what ails U.S. cities and towns. Still, some of these endeavors have met with success and now have become traditions in their own right. More important, festivals, no matter their aims, continue to encourage unstructured and lively interactions among individuals—often individuals who come from different cultural backgrounds. This distinctive characteristic of festivals is inherently valuable and makes them exceptional among the range of commemorative activities in which Americans engage.

NOTES

1. John Bodnar, *Remaking America: Public Memory, Commemoration, and Patriotism in the Twentieth Century* (Princeton, NJ: Princeton University Press, 1992), 13, 14.

2. On historical pageants, see David Glassberg, *American Historical Pageantry: The Uses of Tradition in the Early Twentieth Century* (Chapel Hill: University of North Carolina Press, 1990).

3. Kathleen Neils Conzen, David A. Gerber, Ewa Morawska, George E. Pozzetta, and Rudolph J. Vecoli, "The Invention of Ethnicity: A Perspective from the U.S.A.," *Journal of American Ethnic History* 12, no. 1 (Fall 1992), 3–41.

4. "Pinkster Celebration," *Historic Hudson Valley*, http://www.hudsonvalley. org/education/pinkster. See also, James Fenimore Cooper, *Satanstoe*, chapter 5 http://www.gutenberg.org/files/8880/8880-h/8880-h.htm.

5. Conzen et al., "The Invention of Ethnicity," 17, 24.

6. Bodnar, *Remaking America*, 52.

7. Glassberg, *American Historical Pageantry*, 4.

8. "National Folk Festival History," *National Council for the Traditional Arts*, http://ncta-usa.org/wp/wp-content/uploads/2014/09/NFF-History.pdf.

9. Alan Lomax, "Appeal for Cultural Equity," *The World of Music, Quarterly Journal of the International Music Council (UNESCO)* 14, no. 2 (1972), 3–17.

10. Michael Douma, "Tulip Time and the Invention of a New Dutch American Ethnic Identity," *American Studies* 53, no. 1 (2014), 149. See also, "Tulip Time Festival History," https://www.tuliptime.com/tulip-time-festival-history/.

11. Douma, "Tulip Time and the Invention of a New Dutch American Ethnic Identity," 152.

12. Douma, "Tulip Time and the Invention of a New Dutch American Ethnic Identity,"153.

13. Lon Kurashige, "The Problem of Biculturalism: Japanese American Identity and Festival Before World War II," *Journal of American History* 86 (March 2000), 1634. See also, Lon Kurashige, *Japanese American Celebration and Conflict: A History of Ethnic Identity and Festival, 1934–1990* (Berkeley: University of California Press, 2002).

14. *Nisei Week Japanese Festival*, http://www.niseiweek.org/.

15. Bodnar, *Remaking America,* 54. See also, *Svensk Hyllningsfest*, http://www.svenskhyllningsfest.org/index.html.

16. For a detailed examination of the Bicentennial Festival of American Folklife, see William S. Walker, *A Living Exhibition: The Smithsonian and the Transformation of the Universal Museum* (Amherst: University of Massachusetts Press, 2013), chapter 5.

17. Walker, *A Living Exhibition*, 193.

18. Tammy S. Gordon, *The Spirit of 1976: Commerce, Community, and the Politics of Commemoration* (Amherst: University of Massachusetts Press, 2013).

19. Matthew Frye Jacobson, *Roots Too: White Ethnic Revival in Post-Civil Rights America* (Cambridge, MA: Harvard University Press, 2008).

Figure 4.1. "Gunsmoke," by Ian Livesey, portrays the Sealed Knot at Sizergh Castle, Cumbria. https://creativecommons.org/licenses/by/2.0/.

Chapter 4

Reenactment

Performing the Past

Cathy Stanton

*If you haven't witnessed a historic battle reenactment, or seen bygone
soldiers deliver smoky salvos at open-air museums, then you've probably
seen them lampooned on The Simpsons or South Park or in any number of
books, movies, and other artifacts of the late-twentieth century's seeming
obsession with avocational military reenactment. Like festivals, and often
alongside them, military reenactment—especially of the Civil War—has
become a staple of commemorative life in America. But what meanings
lie within our persistent urge to reanimate these bloody pasts? Seeking
answers, Cathy Stanton joined the fray. What she discovered there will
fascinate heritage professionals looking to engage old constituencies in
new conversations. At issue particularly amid the deep political divides
that characterize life in the early twenty-first century is the possibility,
suggested here, that confronting the commemorative passions of our
nation's graying reenactor corps may shed light on anxieties that concern
all of us.*

—ed.

Some twenty years ago, I put on a blue wool uniform, picked up a fife, and
went off to play war. In my assumed persona as Horace, a young musician
in the Union army, I was trying to gain some inside understanding of a phenomenon I found deeply puzzling but also deeply intriguing: the world of
avocational military reenactment.

Most people—and certainly all who have worked in the realm of historic
preservation or interpretation—have encountered reenactors at some time.
Many observers are initially disturbed by what appears to be a glorification
of war, weapons, and military life, couched within an intense focus, sometimes amounting to obsession, with the minutiae of battle histories, tactics,
and material culture. I portrayed Horace for two years, followed by some

31

subsequent study of Revolutionary War reenactment undertaken for the U.S. National Park Service (NPS) and some later observation of reenactors within the "experience economy" that has been developing in the cultural sector in recent decades.[1] What I discovered is that this form of historical performance serves to negotiate a surprising range of personal and social questions for the people who participate in it. It also overlaps in substantial ways with the professional realm of historic interpretation and preservation, creating both synergies and tensions.

Throughout human history and across cultures, people have reenacted important events—often including violent ones—as a way of orienting themselves in time and space, paying homage to forebears, and constructing community and identity in the present and future. In the modern world, these behaviors have often been linked with nation-building and also with tourism and recreation.

In the specific context of the United States, we can see examples of military reenactment as far back as 1822, when twenty survivors of the fight on Lexington Green helped to represent the event for an audience. The national centennial in 1876 saw many types of historical performance and reenactment, and in the latter part of the nineteenth century, growing nostalgia by and about Civil War veterans prompted a range of reenactment-like activities. Many of these were ritualized performances of reunion and brotherhood by white veterans from the North and the South, an important emotional strategy by which post-Reconstruction white nationalism was facilitated.[2]

As we learned in the previous chapter, during the Progressive era around the turn of the twentieth century, historical pageantry emerged as an extremely popular form of public commemoration that also foreshadowed many aspects of contemporary military reenactment. Pageants sometimes involved hundreds or even thousands of participants and frequently included scenes relating to the nation's wars (but usually without the shooting). Organizers believed that coming together in shared performances of history could help communities and individuals reach a common understanding of citizenship in the face of many changes and competing visions of what it meant to be an American.[3]

Pageantry's vision of the future flowing in a progressive, episodic, orderly way from the past did not survive the shocks of World War I and the Great Depression. But it contributed to a set of conventions for costumed interpretation that were emerging at historic sites around the United States, especially in the eastern states. The "colonial revival" of the early twentieth century and the 1933 shift of battlefield protection from the War Department to the NPS helped expand the history-oriented infrastructure for public recreation and education. Many of these sites focused on what is now most often termed "living history" as opposed to "reenactment," portraying domestic and everyday life rather than military experiences. But the two types of cultural performances were by no means neatly separated. The crafts and folkways revival of the 1930s included groups like the National Muzzle Loading Rifle Association (founded in 1933), which brought together enthusiasts who wanted to use and not merely collect historic weapons. The North-South Skirmish Association (N-SSA), formed in 1950, provided similar opportunities for those with a specific interest in Civil War weaponry. Both groups remain active today.

The form of military reenactment that emerged after World War II was already moving toward the much more holistic, immersive approach that is familiar today. The Civil War centennial (1961–1965) was an important catalyst for contemporary reenactment. High-profile recreations of major battles remained center stage, starting with a depiction of the First Battle of Manassas in 1961 that drew the N-SSA and other hobbyists—including many Korean and World War II veterans—into an uneasy partnership with the NPS and sparked debates about safety and appropriate strategies of commemoration that continue into the present.[4]

During the decade between the end of the Civil War centennial and the start of the national bicentennial, interest in military reenactment dwindled as Americans watched the costly and controversial real war in Vietnam on their television sets. Military culture became a highly polarizing rather than a unifying aspect of U.S. society. By the start of the bicentennial in 1775, the Vietnam War was over, but it had opened troubling questions for many people about national ideals, policies, and history, questions linked with widespread reassessments of power relationships based on race and gender. The younger people—the majority of them men—who took up reenacting during the bicentennial came of age during that turbulent period of questioning, and their experiences shaped and continue to shape the reenactment community in important ways.

During the bicentennial years, reenactors expanded their activities well beyond the peak moments on the battlefield. Weekend encampments started to become more elaborate and multifaceted, with people taking up specialized roles (doctor, politician, well-known generals) and a growing network of "sutlers"—merchants dealing in historically patterned goods—supplying gear both at and outside of events. New quasi-military organizational structures began to take shape at regional and national scales in order to facilitate the daunting logistical challenges of staging multiday gatherings that could involve hundreds and sometimes thousands of participants and spectators. The bicentennial reenactments ended in 1981 with a five-day encampment at Yorktown, Virginia where nearly 200,000 visitors watched 2,500 reenactors stage the British surrender, an event that many reenactors mentioned to me to as an emotional high point after six years of building camaraderie and expertise within their ranks. The Yorktown reenactment was also compelling because the surrender could be staged in a more or less authentic form without violating the NPS's ban on representing actual fighting, a rule that had been in place since the early Civil War centennial battle reenactments.

Following the bicentennial, the reenactor community experienced a boom period in the United States and elsewhere. Revolutionary War reenactment continued to be popular and the Civil War gained in visibility and appeal as well, including in places like Canada, Australia, and many parts of Europe.[5] Popular culture had much to do with this. A spate of high-profile historical films and documentaries (*Glory* in 1989, Ken Burns's *The Civil War* in 1990, *Gettysburg* in 1993) brought tremendous visibility to military histories while also often making use of reenactors themselves as a corps of highly trained, enthusiastic extras. But just as performative forms of commemoration a century before were substantially shaped by the aging of the generation that had fought the Civil War, the late twentieth-century expansion of the reenactor ranks also had a great deal to do with another big bump in American demographics: the maturing of the baby boom generation.

This was the moment at which I entered the reenacting scene in my role as Horace the Yankee fifer. I had just missed the sequence of spectacular events marking the Civil War's 125th anniversary, some of which had topped 10,000 participants, and I was an active participant-observer in the Civil War reenactor community until the start of the 135th anniversary events, which were even larger. I started my inquiries with the big question that most people tend to ask when they first encounter reenactors—"Why do you do this?"—and heard reenactors' standard answers about wanting to educate the public and keep the history of past sacrifices and struggles alive. But as I began to get to know a few people in southern New England units, I also received invitations to step into the scene and experience it from the inside, a common recruiting strategy that happened to suit my research goals extremely well.

My conclusion at the end of that research was that at bottom, military reenactment in the late decades of the twentieth century was very largely a baby boomer phenomenon, responding to the vexed questions about gender, race, class, national identity, and military culture that this generation had grappled with during their youth. In their thirties and forties, boomer reenactors had leisure time and disposable income that they could devote to exploring their relationships to the nation-state, to militarism, and to one another, particularly as those relationships related to gender and masculinity. Their emphasis on educating the public and honoring past soldiers seemed to me to be part and parcel of asserting the importance of patriotic and personal visions that they felt deeply attached to despite—or perhaps because of—the way those visions had been challenged and shaken during their formative years.

Their parents' World War II era experiences loomed large for these Americans. Whether reenactors themselves had ever served in the military during the Vietnam era—and many did, some even in combat, while some had found ways not to—their desire to pay homage to the American military tradition was deep and heartfelt. There were certainly lingering sectionalisms within Civil War reenactment. These could be seen, for example, in Confederate units whose members refused to adopt the widespread practice of wearing the uniform of the other side at times in order to balance forces more realistically in battle depictions. And there were undoubtedly racialized undercurrents in this historically very white hobby. But the community's ready embrace of black Civil War reenactors in the 1990s after the release of *Glory* suggested to me that a shared devotion to the idealized figure of the "ordinary" American citizen-soldier provided crucial common ground and revealed a good deal about the community's fundamental values and motivations.[6]

Reenactors express and enact those values through an ever-more well-elaborated set of languages and conventions centering around the twin poles of safety and authenticity.[7] Over time, the consensus position has continued to move in the direction of ever-more holistic, accuracy-conscious portrayals of the past, with the extreme position staked out by the kind of "hard-core" reenactors that Tony Horwitz profiled—and to some extent lampooned—in his well-known 1998 book *Confederates in the Attic: Dispatches from the Unfinished Civil War*. At the inauthentic extreme are those disparagingly known as "farbs" (a word of uncertain origin), with the great majority of reenactors somewhere in the middle.

Since true accuracy in depicting wars is not desirable even if it were possible, the question of where to draw the line between historical precedent and present-day performance, between actual danger or hardship and a risk-free representation of those experiences, is a hugely important one that reenactors constantly debate. Horwitz's portrait of detail-obsessed hard-cores in search of the next peak experience of time travel does not reflect the thoughtful ways that the reenactor community constructs and patrols this essential distinction between the symbolic and the literal. "Safety is the line," one Civil War reenactor—a combat veteran—told me, describing how his peak moments when "the window opens" between imagined and experienced reality were enabled by the fact that he knew he could make this big emotional shift without actual risk. An organizer and officer in a Revolutionary War "umbrella organization" echoed this idea, saying, "If someone isn't safe, then authenticity doesn't matter." Some scholars of tourism have noted that battlefield tourism similarly serves to mark and reinforce the line between safety and danger. In this view, symbolic and commemorative experiences of war serve a crucial function in helping to define—and perhaps defend—the ordinary, desired, and often fragile state of peace that enables the living of our everyday lives.[8]

In listening to reenactors endlessly parse fine points of material accuracy, I also came to understand the languages of authenticity and safety as a way to create a buffer zone around the larger issues of gender and national identity that seemed to underpin the entire reenactor enterprise. It is not that reenactors obsess about minutiae *instead* of engaging more directly with those questions, but rather that they engage *indirectly*, through the medium of performance. This became clearer to me when I looked in detail at the heated, lengthy debates over whether women should portray soldiers in battle reenactments. Some who opposed the practice used the direct language of the present day. They had purposefully created a male-centered enclave and did not want it invaded by women. But the more nuanced, and ultimately more productive, discussions revolved around performance conventions. Were the women's portrayals convincing? If not—if they were too readily identifiable as women or there was no specific historical example of a disguised woman in their particular regiment—were they being held to higher performance standards than, for example, overweight middle-aged males portraying starving Confederate infantrymen? As the debate unfolded, a consensus position formed around a "35-foot rule" for women passing as male soldiers, along with a tacit admission everyone should be working toward more convincing and historically grounded performances.[9]

The very large 135th Civil War anniversary events around the turn of the century probably saw the peak numbers for the baby boom moment in military reenacting, with the core demographic in the reenactor community entering its fifties and sixties, now finding it more of a stretch to portray field soldiers in terms of both credibility and stamina. The generational shift has meant smaller events, a different personal relationship with national histories and identities, and an interesting intersection with the crowded and image-saturated cultural sector that has been developing since the 1990s. At that intersection, long-standing tensions and synergies between avocational reenactment and the more professionalized worlds of public history and museum interpretation have perhaps been changing as well.

The two realms have never been neatly separated. My survey of Revolutionary War reenactment in relation to the NPS, for example, showed that members of the staff at many national battlefield parks also reenacted avocationally, while many reenactors have worked part- or full-time as interpreters at historic sites. This is perhaps particularly true for the younger cohort of military reenactors, many of whom grew up in the hobby rather than discovering it as adults. There is a natural symbiosis between sites and reenactors: reenactors greatly value original battlefields and historic environments for the resonance and authenticity these places lend to their own experiences, while they offer a reliably eye-catching type of volunteer-led programming that can draw visitors and attention to museums and parks. Tensions often arise around differing approaches to their shared educational and commemorative mission. Reenactors' focus on minutiae and militarism can clash with historic sites' more contextual and sometimes critical approach, a difference that is perhaps most clearly seen in the NPS's emphasis on maintaining a memorial atmosphere at battlefield parks while reenactors insist that their performances *are* an appropriate form of memorial to the soldiers of the past.

Military reenactment is still shaped by the older influences of veterans' rituals and historical pageantry as well as boomer-era practices. But in large part through their partnerships with historic sites, reenactors have also been drawn more deeply into the "experience economy" and what Erika Doss has termed "memorial mania." All historical projects now vie for attention with many other types of digital and actual performances, memorialization, and branding or image-making efforts.

Reenactors were among the most enthusiastic early adopters of digital technologies like listservs, websites, and social media. These tools enabled a kind of "virtual campfire" that extended and enabled the community experiences of actual encampments. But with more and more of social life and historical encounter now taking place through electronic media, reenactors, along with historic sites and professional interpreters, find themselves struggling to defend their more materially based, labor-intensive approach to understanding and presenting the past. Reenactors and historic sites have long produced forms of "augmented reality" that create imagined historical environments and scenarios, but that sense of alternative historical reality is increasingly available to anyone with a computer or a smart phone. Audiences have become familiar with newer forms of historical "edutainment" that include role-playing games and "second-person" scenarios allowing participants to act out particular experiences and fantasies—World War II soldier, fugitive slave, pirate queen. Scott Magelssen has adapted the online gaming term "simming" to describe these types of performances, which blur the lines between reality and make-believe in ever more immersive and technologically mediated ways.

These shifts have pushed all cultural producers to become more entrepreneurial—and often more self-funding and financially precarious—as they work to establish an active presence in a setting shaped by both widely dispersed public input and giant technology corporations through which cultural expression increasingly flows.[10] The short-lived but widely popular Pokémon Go phenomenon in the summer of 2016 showed just how quickly these new forms could change the commemorative landscape. Tens of millions of game players worldwide were suddenly searching for virtual fantasy creatures ("Pokémon") in hybrid real/digital spaces, many of which involved public sites like parks, historic sites, and museums. Visitors were suddenly their own performers at historic sites, with minimal influence by institutions themselves

and little of the kind of face-to-face interactivity that conventional reenactment performances have fostered. Many sites scrambled to attach themselves
to the Pokémon Go bandwagon, despite widespread concern in the traditional
cultural sector about issues of distraction and safety. But internal debates
were moot; the craze ended almost as quickly as it began, leaving IRL ("in
real life") historical interpreters somewhat dazed and confused.[11] As both
professional and avocational interpreters work to capture attention in this
new environment, they may find themselves discovering more commonalities and reshaping their relationship with each other, helping to reinvent this
performance form once more.

NOTES

1. My study of Civil War reenactment in the mid-1990s can be found in "Being
the Elephant: The American Civil War Reenacted," unpublished master's thesis, Vermont College of Norwich University, 1997, available online at www.cathystanton.
net. Study of Revolutionary War reenactment undertaken for the NPS can be found
in "Reenactors in the Parks: A Study of External Revolutionary War Reenactment
Activity at National Parks," Boston Support Office, Northeast Ethnography Program,
National Park Service, 1999, also available online through www.nps.gov.

2. On battle commemoration at Lexington and Concord, see Edward T. Linenthal, *Sacred Ground: Americans and Their Battlefields* (Urbana and Chicago: University of Illinois Press, 1991), 9–51. On post–Civil War performative commemoration,
see Linenthal, *Sacred Ground*, 87–126; Stuart McConnell, *Glorious Contentment:
The Grand Army of the Republic, 1865–1900* (Chapel Hill and London: University of
North Carolina Press, 1992); and Nina Silber, *The Romance of Reunion: Northerners
and the South, 1865–1900* (Chapel Hill and London: University of North Carolina
Press, 1993).

3. On the pageant movement, see David Glassberg, *American Historical Pageantry: The Uses of Tradition in the Early Twentieth Century* (Chapel Hill and London: University of North Carolina Press, 1990).

4. On Civil War centennial reenactments, see Jay Anderson, *Time Machines: The
World of Living History* (Nashville, TN: American Association for State and Local
History, 1984), especially "Civil Wars," 141–143; and Linenthal, *Sacred Ground*,
97–103.

5. Although this chapter focuses specifically on American reenactment and wars,
there are also substantial communities of avocational military reenactors in these and
other places, often devoted to place-specific conflicts like the English Civil War or
the Napoleonic wars. World War I has not seemed to draw as much attention from
reenactors as other wars, but World War II reenacting has become increasingly
popular in recent decades, perhaps linked with "great generation" nostalgia in much
the same way that the aging of the Civil War generation in late nineteenth-century
America prompted widespread veneration and commemoration. For an ethnographic

study of reenactment of more recent eras, see Jenny Thompson, *War Games: Inside the World of 20th-Century War Reenactors* (Washington, DC: Smithsonian Books, 2010).

6. On the integration of black reenactors into the virtually all-white hobby, see Stephen Belyea and Cathy Stanton, "'Their Time Will Yet Come': The African American Presence in Civil War Reenactment," in Martin Blatt, Tom Brown, and Donald Yacovone, eds. *Hope and Glory: Essays on the Legacy of the 54th Massachusetts Regiment* (University of Massachusetts Press, 2001), 253–274.

7. For thoughtful discussions of discourses of authenticity within living history performances, see Richard Handler and Eric Gable, *The New History in an Old Museum: Creating the Past at Colonial Williamsburg* (Durham, NC: Duke University Press, 1997); Barbara Kirshenblatt-Gimblett, "Plimoth Plantation," in *Destination Culture: Tourism, Museums, and Heritage* (Berkeley: University of California Press, 1998), 189–200; and Scott Magelssen, "Tourist Performance in the Twenty-first Century," in Scott Magelssen and Rhona Justice-Malloy, eds. *Enacting History* (Tuscaloosa: University Press of Alabama, 2011), 174–202.

8. See, for example, Debbie Lisle, "Consuming Danger: Reimagining the War/Tourism Divide," *Alternatives: Global, Local, Political* 25 (2000), 91–116.

9. For discussion of women reenacting in soldier roles, see Jim Cullen, "Patriotic 'Gore': Jonathan Clarke's Civil War," in *The Civil War in Popular Culture* (Washington: Smithsonian Institution Press, 1995), 172–199; and Cathy Stanton, *Being the Elephant: The American Civil War Reenacted*, 102–119.

10. "Experience economy" was coined in the 1990s by marketing theorists B. Joseph Pine II and James H. Gilmore to describe the increasingly purposeful marketing of experience as a component of brand- and place-promotion. See *The Experience Economy* (Cambridge, MA: Harvard Business Review Press, 2011[1999]). On "memorial mania," see Erika Doss, *Memorial Mania: Public Feeling in America* (Chicago: University of Chicago Press, 2010). On "simming," see Scott Magelssen, *Simming: Participatory Performance and the Making of Meaning* (Ann Arbor: University of Michigan Press, 2014). On precarity within the cultural sector, with a particular emphasis on professional living historians including military reenactors, see Amy Tyson, *The Wages of History: Emotional Labor on Public History's Front Lines* (Boston and Amherst: University of Massachusetts Press, 2013) as well as Handler and Gable, *The New History in an Old Museum*, particularly "Picket Lines," 208–219.

11. On museums' reaction to Pokémon Go, see Andrea Peterson, "Holocaust Museum to Visitors: Please Stop Catching Pokémon Here," *Washington Post*, July 12, 2016, and Nadja Sayej, "American Art Museums Cautiously Embrace Pokémon Go," *The Guardian*, July 19, 2016.

Figure 5.1.   An enthusiastic crowd gathers around Plymouth Rock during the waterfront redevelopment for the Pilgrim Tercentenary of 1920. Courtesy Pilgrim Hall Museum, Plymouth, Massachusetts.

Chapter 5

A Local Commemoration
of National Significance

Anne C. Reilly

Moving forward from our survey of modern commemorative forms, Anne C. Reilly introduces a new consideration: scope. What, from a planning standpoint, are the key considerations bearing on commemoration that is primarily local in outlook? Or national? Or even global? How do we manage when the lines, as so often is the case, are not clearly drawn? It is this question especially that frames Reilly's fascinating account of efforts during the early part of the last century to commemorate the Pilgrims' landing at Plymouth Rock. Pilgrim mythology had grown so pervasive throughout the nation that Plymoutheans found themselves unable to control commemorative goings on right in their own backyards. Reilly's is a cautionary tale about the weighing of historical significance, the pitfalls of private funding, and the dangers of abandoning the present for the past. Will organizers of Plymouth's upcoming quadricentennial learn from their predecessors' missteps? Reilly concludes with guidance for their path, and advice for those of us who work among the nation's most cherished historical places.

—ed.

In 1912, Arthur Lord petitioned the trustees of the Pilgrim Society for the authority to appoint a committee that would be responsible for outlining the plan and scope of the celebration of the 300th anniversary of the Pilgrims' landing at Plymouth, Massachusetts, in 1620. The Society, founded in 1820 at the time of this momentous event's bicentennial, sought to preserve and protect the memory of the English colonists. Lord, the Society's president, urged the trustees to consider how the town could permanently mark the significance of the event, predicting that national patriotic and hereditary societies would want to take advantage of the tercentenary and erect physical memorials at the landing site on the town's waterfront. Any redevelopment plan, he cautioned, should "not unduly interfere with the necessary uses which this community make of the water front." A successful memorial park would benefit the people of Plymouth and "at the same time present to the visitors a more attractive environment and one more suggestive of the scene which we seek there to commemorate."[1]

Lord recognized the need to balance the national significance of the tercentenary with its local setting and played a key role in steering the commemoration. With roots in the local community, he also wielded influence on a state level, and successfully articulated the Pilgrims' national significance. A native of Plymouth, Lord graduated from Harvard and practiced law in Boston and in Plymouth. During his career, he served in the Massachusetts Legislature and as vice president of the American Bar Association and president of the Massachusetts Bar Association. In addition to being president of the Pilgrim Society, in the years leading up to 1920, he placed himself in positions that would allow him to wield influence on the development of Plymouth, including serving as the chairman of the town's planning board.[2] Lord possessed a clear vision for the tercentenary and he was able to eloquently garner support for it. He was also willing to pour an incredible amount of his own time and energy into coordinating the commemoration. However, despite Lord's involvement, the tercentenary did not always meet the needs of the Plymouth community. Although plans originated within the town itself, the broader appeal of the commemoration led to the involvement of state and federal commissions and, over time, dependency on funding from these external sources eclipsed the community's role. This and other facets of Plymouth's tercentenary story make it a perfect case study of the challenges of orchestrating a local commemoration of an event with national significance.

During the Colonial Revival, major anniversaries provided catalysts for grand commemorations staged at the sites of historic events. These commemorations reflected the preoccupations of individuals and groups who wanted to harness the power of heritage to address concerns they faced in the late nineteenth and early twentieth centuries. Commemorators wanted to root American identity in Anglo-Saxonism, Protestantism, and representative government. And they used history to bolster their claims to authority in the present. The need to teach American values to the nation's citizens seemed extremely urgent to many white Americans in this period, as immigration reached record levels and new political ideologies, particularly socialism, seemed to threaten American democracy. The tercentenary of the Pilgrim landing drew national attention, because since the mid-nineteenth century, it had been promoted as a birthplace of the nation and a source of inspiration for "true" Americans.

Plymouth was an active community with a population of 13,045 in 1920.[3] It was a diverse town, stretching from small agricultural villages in the south to working-class neighborhoods surrounding the Cordage Company, one of the world's leading rope-making manufactories, in the North. The heart of the Plymouth community was the downtown area nestled on the waterfront. Water Street, which ran along the harbor, was home to declining shipping and fishing endeavors. The old wharves and counting houses still stood on the shore near the power plant owned by the Plymouth Electric Company. The Pilgrims landed at a site on this waterfront and many observers, who saw nothing inspiring in an industrial landscape, felt its "discreditable appearance" detracted from the Pilgrim legacy.[4]

In response to these local conditions, some commemorators called for a cultural and international exposition to be held in Boston instead. The 1876 Centennial Exhibition in Philadelphia ushered in a period of world's fairs held to commemorate historic anniversaries in the United States, including the Columbian Exposition held in Chicago in 1893 to commemorate the 400th anniversary of Columbus' arrival in the New World. Virginia commemorated the 1907 tercentenary of the settlement of Jamestown (that other birthplace of America) with an international exposition at Norfolk. Many people, including Massachusetts Governor Samuel W. McCall, anticipated that the 300th anniversary of the Pilgrim landing would be a perfect opportunity to hold a similarly grand display in Boston.[5] Others objected to holding yet another world's fair and protested that such a celebration would scandalize those it meant to honor.[6] Their view of the Pilgrims as God-fearing, home-loving, humble people did not fit with the commercialization of a grand exposition. The existence of multiple memorial visions testifies to the malleable potency of the Pilgrim story.

Ultimately, the state focused its efforts on making permanent improvements to historic areas in Plymouth and holding a grand historical pageant to celebrate the Pilgrim legacy. The federal government appropriated $300,000 for making alterations to Plymouth's landscape, while the state of Massachusetts secured a similar amount for the historical pageant and other commemorative events.[7] The Massachusetts Pilgrim Tercentenary Commission, which the General Court authorized in 1916 to determine a plan for the commemoration, called for clearing the area around Plymouth Rock and the early graveyard on Burial Hill.[8] The commemorators wanted to transform the landing site of the Pilgrims into sacred ground. They hoped that once reinvented—both physically and in the popular imagination—the Plymouth waterfront would become a shrine for modern American pilgrims. They believed that by altering the landscape they could produce patriotism; the physical space would inspire visitors to emulate the colonists.

Carrying out these plans proved difficult, especially following the country's entry into World War I. The redevelopment stalled as the nation directed its energy overseas in 1917 and 1918. Following the war, the commemorators had even more reasons to celebrate the Pilgrim story: emphasizing a shared Anglo-American heritage reinforced the wartime alliance with Great Britain, while promoting the Pilgrims as America's first capitalists offered a historic precedent during the postwar Red Scare. However, grandiose schemes proposed before the war had to be scaled back due to fewer funds and the increased cost of materials. Consequently, the state could not create a cohesive memorial landscape as proposed in 1917. Instead, they had to rely more on the generosity of individuals and interest groups to erect smaller memorials, which led to competition over who would erect the most prominent monument. Thirteen patriotic and hereditary organizations erected memorials in Plymouth for the tercentenary, each with different goals, different budgets, and different styles. It was a huge challenge to coordinate these projects. Moreover, the infusion of so much outside money removed aesthetic control from local hands.

The interests of the out-of-town boosters of Pilgrim heritage often diverged from those of the local businesspeople and residents. By focusing on how to best make Plymouth a shrine to the Pilgrims, the state commemorators overlooked the day-to-day needs of a living community. They assumed that Plymoutheans would jump at the opportunity to destroy a landscape that had, until recently, been the economic heart of their town. Once the land on the waterfront (now Pilgrim Memorial State Park) became the state's property, any memorials erected on it had to be approved by the state art commission, rather than the town. Often the concerns of local landowners, businesspeople, and town leaders went unheeded in the torrent of suggestions from state and federal commission members, outside commemorators, preservationists, and architects. These negotiations delayed the completion of the waterfront redevelopment. Visitors attending the tercentenary pageant in the summer of 1921 would have seen a barren waterfront, cleared of wharves and shipping buildings, but not yet a beautifully landscaped park. The new portico over the fabled Plymouth Rock, donated by the Colonial Dames of America, was not dedicated until November 29, 1921.

The permanent memorials erected in Plymouth were largely the gifts of outsiders and represented the memory of the Pilgrims that political and cultural elites wanted to promote. The townspeople of Plymouth also contributed to the tercentenary, although in more ephemeral ways.[9] The Town Tercentenary Committee, the Plymouth Selectmen, and the Chamber of Commerce orchestrated the details of hosting thousands of visitors. They urged the people of Plymouth to display the American flag on homes and businesses as often as weather permitted during the spring and summer. According to them, "American flags everywhere will indicate the real significance of the Tercentenary Celebration as marking an epoch in the life of the Nation and not simply an event of local importance as it might seem to those who do not entirely grasp."[10] Plymoutheans were told cleaning, painting, gardening, hanging bunting, and decorating homes and cars were ways to support their town while it was in the national spotlight.[11]

The residents of Plymouth and other local communities also rose to the challenge of producing the pageant sponsored by the state commission. *The Pilgrim Spirit,* written and directed by Harvard University professor George P. Baker, depicted scenes of early European exploration of New England, the experiences of the Separatists in England and Holland, and the settlement of the colony. Baker portrayed the Pilgrims as the authors of American religious and civil liberty, illuminating a path followed by Washington, Lincoln, and other American heroes.[12] People from Plymouth, Kingston, Duxbury, and Marshfield performed in the pageant as actors or as members of the 240-voice chorus. The cast included not only Pilgrim descendants and community leaders but also members of Plymouth's immigrant population. Local residents also built props—from muskets to a Norse galley—and sewed 1,100 costumes from 13,000 yards of material. The Boy Scouts of Plymouth served as ushers during performances.

This community participation extended to other commemorative events. President Harding visited Plymouth on August 1, 1921, drawing an estimated 100,000 visitors to the town for the day. He was greeted by a large parade that featured floats designed and built by residents. Some of these residents had not been given space in the official commemoration but tied their own heritage to the Pilgrim story. The Plymouth Portuguese National Club, for example, built a float that depicted the explorer Vasco da Gama in the ship *St. Gabriel.* The float also included images of a Pilgrim, a Native American, George Washington, Abraham Lincoln, and World War I veterans, with a banner proclaiming "Liberty." A commentator noted that the "crowds were quick to catch the spirit of the float . . . it was America and Americanism."[13]

In addition to participating in the pageant and the parade, some Plymoutheans created their own programs, including the Pilgrim Progress, which would become an annual tradition. The Progress featured costumed individuals, representing each survivor of the Pilgrims' first winter. They marched through town to the crest of Burial Hill, where a short service of hymns and readings would be completed at the site of the Pilgrims' fort. From June 20 to September 8, the modern-day Pilgrims made their progress every day, except Sundays, holidays, and pageant nights. One of the organizers, Dr. Harold C. Ernst, who taught at Harvard University Medical School, explained, "The underlying motive of the whole was to have something distinctly characteristic of early Plymouth life as part of the tercentennial celebration—and that this should be under local control." The planners originally envisioned that all those who took part would be *Mayflower* descendants, but the logistics of such an endeavor made them open it to "all who reverence the Pilgrims."[14] Cleaning their town, feeding visitors, participating in the pageant or other commemorative events—this is how local residents commemorated the 300th anniversary, even as they lost control of the physical redevelopment of their community.

One hundred years after the tercentenary, Plymoutheans are again preparing for a major commemoration of the Pilgrim landing. Changes in American culture and society have, not surprisingly, altered our vision of the colonial past. Plymouth 400, Inc., the nonprofit organization in charge of planning the commemoration for 2020, makes it very clear that this is not a "celebration" of the triumph of Anglo-American culture and seeks to show greater sensitivity to the Native American perspective of English colonization.[15] By focusing on cultural interaction between the Wampanoag and English settlers, for instance, the organizers hope to provide opportunities for other previously neglected stories to be heard. However, comparing the 300th and 400th anniversaries can help us understand the dynamics of local commemorations, wherever and whenever they take place. In fact, Plymouth's story presents us with a set of questions that would-be commemorators must confront even today:

WHAT CAN WE LEARN FROM SIMILAR COMMEMORATIONS?

In the case of Plymouth, both generations of commemoration planners looked for models in Jamestown, Virginia, where celebrations in 1907 and 2007 marked the establishment there of the first permanent English settlement in the Americas. The organizers of the Plymouth tercentenary, for example, considered Jamestown's 1907 international exposition but ultimately rejected it for their own purposes. The organizers of Plymouth 400, however, developed a series of "signature events" very much influenced by Jamestown 2007. Considering past commemorations is wise, though planners must be careful not to replicate the divisions that, in the case of Plymouth, pitted some residents against town boosters.

WHAT ARE THE BENEFITS OF COMMEMORATION?

While today's commemorators may not unreservedly celebrate the Pilgrims, they do depend on broader arguments about the benefits of commemorations that were employed at the time of the tercentenary. They emphasize that the anniversary is a tool for economic growth, anticipating the revenue from increased tourism and the consumerism that will accompany it. To be able to successfully carry out their programs for 2020, Plymouth 400, Inc. must secure funding from the government as well as from major corporate sponsors. The long-term economic incentive remains foremost in their presentations to state and federal leaders.[16] But what of stakeholders for whom economic growth is not a priority? Or for those who imagine different paths to profit? Plymouth's story reveals that failing to blaze an inclusive commemorative path jeopardizes proceeds just as it undermines public memory.

HOW CAN WE INSPIRE ENTHUSIASM?

Commemoration requires the involvement of individuals who can find common cause among local celebrants and the state, federal, and private sponsors that support them. Arthur Lord provided important leadership during the tercentenary. Rev. Peter J. Gomes played a similar role until his death in 2011. Born in Plymouth, Gomes was Pusey Minister of Memorial Church at Harvard University. He had a deep love for his hometown's history and had served as president of the Pilgrim Society. He provided a powerful voice for the commemoration as chairman of Plymouth's 400th Anniversary Committee. Commemoration cannot succeed without the guidance of passionate and committed individuals like Lord and Gomes, and yet individuals alone cannot devise a truly inclusive commemorative vision. Activating enthusiasm at all levels of commemorative planning, therefore, is essential.

WHAT IS THE APPROPRIATE MODE
OF COMMEMORATION?

The primary legacy of the tercentenary was the creation of a memorial landscape in Plymouth. There seems to be little motivation to erect new monuments in 2020, perhaps because Plymouth's landscape is already cluttered with them. This may also reflect a shift away from physical memorialization in American commemorative practices. However, for both anniversaries, the first impulse from local leaders was to clean up the community, to make the site welcoming to modern visitors. The Town of Plymouth is currently working on infrastructure improvements to support millions of guests while Plymouth 400 hopes to develop commemorative events featuring special guests and celebrities who will draw a crowd. Accommodating visitors is critical, but it can never come at the expense of residents whose lives are interwoven with the public memory on display. People, after all, are the place.

WHAT IS THE TARGET AUDIENCE?

The organizers of both commemorations in Plymouth never limited the audience to local residents. The goal remains to draw larger crowds from across the nation—or the world. This raises many other demands for housing, transportation, parking, and entertainment. A lesson from the tercentenary is that appealing so much to outsiders can limit a commemoration's appeal to local residents—especially when money is coming from outside sources and streets become clogged with traffic. During the tercentenary local groups planned their own programs to commemorate the tercentenary. These grassroots efforts were essential for providing a full experience for visitors and educating people on different aspects of Plymouth's history. Plymouth 400 is seeking to engage the community by recruiting volunteers and partnering with local organizations and businesses. These partners are encouraged to put on events of their own that connect to the themes of the commemoration.

Finally, the story of Plymouth shows us that commemoration is a process, and one that *always* provokes discussion, if not conflict. Commemorators should neither be surprised by the plethora of proposals, nor discouraged by an inability to reconcile all of them. Each of us interprets and uses the past to meet our needs in the present. Instead of assuming that we all agree on the meaning or importance of an event or person, we should be intentional about asking some difficult questions about the goals and scope of the commemoration and how they will impact the community. These conversations will take *time*—a commodity that commemorators run out of all too often.

NOTES

1. Arthur Lord, report to the Pilgrim Society Trustees, n.d., box 8b, Pilgrim Society Archives, Plymouth, MA. This manuscript is undated. However, a letter to Arthur Lord in the same box indicates that he presented his report at the Trustees Meeting on June 15, 1912. At this meeting, the Trustees voted that he be allowed to appoint a committee to consider the scope of the commemoration.

2. "Arthur Lord, Lawyer, Dies in Boston at 74," *New York Times,* April 11, 1925.

3. Department of Commerce, U.S. Bureau of the Census, *Abstract of the Fourteenth Census of the United States 1920* (Washington, DC: Government Printing Office, 1923), 60. Plymouth is the county seat of Plymouth County, which in 1920 had a population of 156,968 and an area of 675 square miles. It is the largest town in southeastern Massachusetts.

4. *Old Colony Memorial,* February 25, 1921.

5. "McCall Urges Fair on Pilgrims' Anniversary," *Boston Morning Journal,* March 30, 1916.

6. "The Pilgrims' Tercentenary," *New York Times,* February 13, 1914.

7. "To Reset Plymouth Rock," *New York Times,* September 15, 1920.

8. Massachusetts Pilgrim Tercentenary Commission, *Report of the Pilgrim Tercentenary Commission* (Boston, MA: Wright and Potter Printing Company, 1917), 5.

9. For more discussion on the tension between official and local/vernacular memorialization practices, see John Bodnar, *Remaking America: Public Memory, Commemoration, and Patriotism in the Twentieth Century* (Princeton, NJ: Princeton University Press, 1992).

10. "Show the Flag," *Old Colony Memorial,* May 27, 1921.

11. A cartoon in the *Old Colony Memorial* depicted an army of ordinary men, women, and children with brooms, paintbrushes, and rakes at attention. It told readers "Your Town Needs You" and "Don't Be a Slacker." "Your Town Needs You," *Old Colony Memorial,* April 15, 1921.

12. George P. Baker, *The Pilgrim Spirit* (Boston, MA: Marshall Jones Company, 1921). The script included verses by the poets Hermann Hagedorn, Edward Arlington Robinson, Josephine Preston Peabody, and a young Robert Frost. The music was specially composed by George W. Chadwick, Arthur Foote, and John Powell, among others, with orchestrations by Stanislaus Gallo and music by the Gallo Symphony Band of Boston.

13. *Boston Evening Transcript,* August 1, 1921, quoted in Udo J. Hebel, "Historical Bonding with an Expiring Heritage: Revisiting the Plymouth Tercentenary Festivities of 1920/21," in Jurgen Heideking, Genevieve Fabre, and Kai Dreisbach, eds. *Celebrating Ethnicity and Nation: American Festive Culture from the Revolution to the Early 20th Century* (New York: Berghahn Books, 2001), 285.

14. "Summer Days at Plymouth," *Boston Transcript,* July 14, 1921; from the papers of Harold C. Ernst, Massachusetts Historical Society, Boston. The idea for the Progress, which was first suggested by Russell Whitman, came from a letter from Isaac de Rasiere who visited Plymouth in 1627 and reported, "They assemble by beat of drum, each with his firelock in front of the captain's door; they have their cloaks on, and place themselves in order, three abreast, and are lead by a sergeant without beat of drum."

15. See http://www.plymouth400inc.org.

16. Frank Mand, "Little Sign of State Support for Plymouth's 400," *Old Colony Memorial,* April 2, 2016.

Figure 6.1.   Get Territorial: Idaho at 150 capitol steps kick-off event, March 4, 2014.
Michelle Wallace, Idaho State Historical Society.

Chapter 6

Get Territorial
Idaho at 150

Janet L. Gallimore

Knowing what problems to avoid is, of course, essential for planning a successful commemorative event. But what about the scores of practical concerns that confront would-be commemorators? In this essay, Janet L. Gallimore brings a career of experience in cultural programming to bear on the challenge of building a statewide commemorative campaign from the ground up. Gallimore did precisely that along with the Idaho State Historical Society beginning in 2010, just two years into what turned out to be one of the worst global financial crises since the Great Depression. Based as it was on creative partnerships, digital outreach, cooperation with state government, and careful branding, Gallimore's strategy offers more than just a template for organizations seeking to replicate her success. It provides a study in best practices for commemorative planning in an era of fiscal and political uncertainty.

—ed.

Honoring the memory of a person, event, or place demonstrates acknowledgment and respect. It can also serve many concurrent purposes, including using a commemorative opportunity as a catalyst for creating a common voice, in this case for history. It was with this in mind that I and the Idaho State Historical Society embarked in 2010 to mark Idaho's Territorial Sesquicentennial, a dynamic era that began with the Idaho Territorial Act, signed by President Lincoln on March 4, 1863, and one that led to the formation of much of the infrastructure that Idaho enjoys today: post offices, highways, railroads, schools, the court system, water rights, universities, and more. A case could be made that the twenty-seven-year territorial era was the most important period in Idaho history in terms of shaping the state we know today. However, when we began planning for *Get Territorial: Idaho at 150,* Idaho was experiencing crushing budget cuts, and there was no appetite for funding special projects and commissions. We knew that success would hinge on taking an innovative approach. In this chapter, I describe how we did it.

Get Territorial ran from its kick-off on March 4, 2013, to March 4, 2014. Making it a success required that we work with the governor to generate grassroots support driven by mass branding. By involving state agencies in a core planning team while engaging federal, local, and tribal jurisdictions as well as nonprofit organizations, *Get Territorial* made powerful claims for public memory despite a host of challenges.

From the outset, our goals included establishing the State Historical Society's leadership of the commemorative effort to promote history and maintain high visibility. We wanted also to unite the Society's various departments, including the State Historical Museum, State Archives, State Historical Preservation Office, and Historic Sites to create engaging programs and exhibitions. And we wanted to advance history and its brand through statewide promotion and donor investment. Outcomes included enhancing our state by helping people of all ages learn about and appreciate the territorial roots of contemporary Idaho. We aimed to create economic opportunities through heritage tourism. And we wanted to empower Idahoans to learn more about Idaho's history in order to create lasting legacies in their respective communities. Along the way, we sought out models that could be adapted for our purposes. Territorial Sesquicentennial commemorations that inspired us included those from the Kansas and Minnesota Historical Societies. These programs achieved broad statewide engagement and did so, in part, by delivering content affordably on the web.

Early on we formed a task force with a whole host of public agencies that met monthly to craft a performance framework and action plan. Together the task force members nuanced and leveraged existing programs and budgets to create a palette of offerings that ranged from traveling exhibitions, to a "big read" of books from the era, heritage artist events, school curriculum, and a themed scenic byways programs.[1] And yet, Idaho is big. The diagonal distance between where Idaho touches Canada, near Sandpoint to where it touches Utah, near Franklin is almost the same distance as between New York and Chicago. To expand our reach and motivate people across our state to get involved, we had to harness online tools and engage participants with easy ways to get involved. Promotion and marketing of *Get Territorial* were organized by the State Historical Society, in partnership with Red Sky Public Relations. We created a logo, brand attributes, messaging, and a marketing plan, and with the assistance of the Idaho Department of Tourism and the Drake Cooper ad agency, created a state-hosted central web-based calendar to make it easy for any entity to promote its activities.

Creating a digital infrastructure, however, was not enough. Toward providing statewide partners with online content, we developed a promotional toolkit with adaptable templates and made it available for free download from the Society's website. This free marketing toolkit included a letter from the Governor and the Society's executive director; logos for collateral and web applications; and templates for creating banners, advertisements, press releases, and rack cards. We even provided free image downloads and sample language for communities eager to issue commemorative proclamations. A list of frequently asked questions with answers concerning key dates, people, and places of sesquicentennial significance rounded out the package, along with advice concerning technical facets of commemorative events including "fifteen things to do in your community" and a range of suggested interpretive themes.

With all of this, and even despite the economic recession triggered by the Financial Crisis of 2008, we raised nearly $500,000 for numerous State Historical Society exhibitions, publications, and programs.[2] Particular successes included our Capitol Steps kick-off event; partnership with the Idaho Lottery to create a "Great Idaho Cash Word" scratch-off ticket; our collaboration with the Office of First Lady Lori Otter to create *Ida Visits 150 years of Idaho;* the creation of a permanent exhibition on Abraham Lincoln at our Idaho State Archives; a special exhibition titled "Essential Idaho: 150 Things that Make the Gem State Unique;" and a special feature of the Idaho Territory Act under the direction of the Archivist of the United States in the President's room at the U.S. Capitol.

With our task force and representatives from the governor's office and legislative leadership, we crafted a compelling kick-off event on the Capitol steps. The formal entry by all members of the legislature, the Supreme Court justices, constitutional officers, and the governor and First Lady was visually stunning. The program was intentionally crafted to celebrate Idaho's diverse people. The invocation came from a Hispanic Catholic priest, a resounding rendition of *America the Beautiful* was emotionally rendered by an African American legislator, the Shoshone-Paiute Sweet Sage drummers and songs were ethereal, and benediction featured a Nez Perce spiritual leader. The Idaho National Guard presented flags with great decorum. Governor Otter and legislative leadership recognized the value that history brings to our contemporary life. Children's performances provided great joy and a glimpse of our future. With an incredible sponsorship by local KTVB news that created a special feature story that ran weeks in advance of the kick-off, and the statewide broadcast support of Idaho Public television, this event had incredible reach and impact. Over 1,500 people attended and we generated $355,000 of earned media coverage, which extended our impact to a 1.9 million media reach in Idaho, Utah, and Washington.

One of our most novel partnerships was with the Idaho State Lottery Commission, which created a "150" branded lottery ticket and promoted *Get Territorial* at its over 800 retail monitor locations and on its website. The "Great Idaho Cashword" featured a crossword puzzle comprising Idaho history "Fun Facts" that were vetted by our state historian. In two months, Idaho Lottery's "Great Idaho Cash Word" had sold almost 50 percent of its tickets. By the end of the game, it had generated nearly $1,000,000 in direct benefits to Idahoans, including more than $750,000 in benefits to public education and the permanent buildings of Idaho and another $220,000 in retail commissions for Idaho's businesses.

On an entirely different front, we enjoyed a close partnership with the Office of Idaho's First Lady. Lori Otter is a former teacher, education advocate, and author of a children's book series about "Ida," a young girl named after Idaho whose adventures lead her to the state Capitol and throughout its counties. In conjunction with *Get Territorial,* the State Historical Society created a history-focused volume for this popular series. The occasion to work with the First Lady on *Ida Visits 150 Years of Idaho* was a great benefit. It allowed her insight into the expertise of our agency and the breadth of state collections, and it offered us access to a new set of sponsors. Building trust with the First Lady and delivering on results in a timely manner was vital as it earned us her support for our planning of a new State Historical Museum, which will open in 2018. The First Lady has been a significant advocate for this museum and how it will be an essential part of achieving Idaho's educational goals. She has been extremely helpful in lending visibility to this legacy project of the State of Idaho and a critical part of our Foundation for Idaho History capital campaign team.

Idaho's Territorial Sesquicentennial also inspired collector and former Lieutenant Governor David Leroy to bequest his collection to the State Historical Society, and to request that the materials be made available to school children, families, and the public via a permanent exhibition. The collection is arguably the most significant grouping of contemporary artifacts ever assembled relating to the relationship of Abraham Lincoln to Idaho and the Rocky Mountain West. State Archives staff creatively envisioned the opportunity to convert prime areas of the state archives' public space to exhibitions that could provide unrestricted educational access to this signature collection of material. Visitors enter the exhibition through a reconstruction of the Lincoln-era Cabinet Room where President Lincoln signed the Emancipation Proclamation in the White House. Four more exhibition galleries explore the chronological and topical depiction of Lincoln's life, achievements, and relations with the West. Lincoln himself was a youth with no advantage. His poverty, lack of education, broken home status, and subsequent rise to become a great leader and humanitarian make him the perfect role model for today's youth and society.

Our special territorial exhibition, hosted at the Idaho State Museum, featured a comprehensive telling of Idaho's story, created through input from Idaho's tribes, cities, communities and citizens. "Essential Idaho: 150 Things that Make the Gem State Unique" was an amazing statewide, grassroots engagement effort that built relationships and trust in our Agency. Museums and communities throughout the state were proud to have their community and artifacts featured in the Capital City. These relationships were vital as we began the formal planning and statewide engagement process for our new Idaho State Museum, a $16.9 million reimagining of our Museum, which opens in 2018.

Finally, the sesquicentennial celebrations also inspired U.S. senators Jim Risch (Boise) and Mike Crapo (Idaho Falls) to connect Idaho history to our Nation's Capital. Under the watchful eye of the Archivist of the United States, the Idaho Territorial Act, signed by President Lincoln, was escorted to the White House's ornate President's Room. On March 4, 2013, 150 years to the day when and in the room where President Abraham Lincoln signed the Idaho Territory Act, our Senators live streamed their presentation and interpretation of this extraordinarily rare volume to the public.

Successful though it was, our *Get Territorial* task force did face challenges. While the Idaho State Historical Society led the effort and our partners marshaled existing resources, we had no one person who served as a project manager. This meant that all parties had to be self-reliant to meet their respective goals and track their own results. There was no central data collection effort, so it was difficult to articulate the collective impact of what was happening at the local level. From testimonials and media accounts, we knew that there were many statewide activities. It was clear to us that, during the year of the commemoration, the history community spoke with a single voice and made great use of the toolkit that we provided. And yet, unfortunately, we were not in the position to gather data sufficient to create a meaningful statewide impact statement. Similarly, although the relationships formed by our task force garnered a strong network, we did not have a formal method to sustain these relationships past the initial year of the commemoration. Fortunately, one highly engaged legislator created an "Idaho Day" initiative as a legacy of *Get Territorial*. A small contingent of state agencies of the original task force continue to work together on this annual one-day event.

The lack of a dedicated, formal budget and commission was both a blessing and a serious weakness. It was a great opportunity to demonstrate to State of Idaho Officials that state agencies could be entrepreneurial, responsive, and team oriented. However, state agencies were already overburdened with their required work. Adding the expectation of a statewide commemoration was often overwhelming and really could not be optimized. In addition to the value a defined budget would have brought to the initiative, a formal, appointed commission would also have contributed validity and "clout" that our staff-led effort simply could not. This surely would have contributed to the opportunity to expand our fundraising and promotional capacity.

Overall, the activities championed and led by the State Historical Society did achieve our intended outcomes by encouraging people across the state to learn about and appreciate the territorial roots of contemporary Idaho, often by getting involved in their respective communities. Perhaps equally important, we had the opportunity to demonstrate the value of history by articulating how the efforts of citizens and elected officials of that era built the cornerstones of Idaho today. The context provided by making these connections resonated deeply. Each year during our state appropriations hearing, I present a special story or object of Idaho's past that connects the legislature with state government history. When asked if I should change this annual tradition, the committee cochairs assured me that the body not only enjoys the learning this action provides but also reminds them truly of the impact of their respective roles today and the vital importance of their decision making on Idaho's future.

Idaho, like many large rural states, comprises a cadre of very small communities, each with their own distinct identity. Rallying around stories of people and places at the community level has tremendous power. Preserving and honoring special places generates pride and creates distinctive community amenities. Commemorative events can provide a great opportunity to involve citizens, organizations, funders, and stakeholders, engage in topics of contemporary importance, view them through the lens of history, and use that perspective to make informed decisions. Commemorations can also serve as the foundation for future initiatives that build a collective narrative for citizens, communities, and America. *Get Territorial* sought to do just that by providing a strong and purposeful voice for history. Through partnerships, strategic messaging, and systematic engagement, this voice was heard clearly over the course of an entire year. Connections developed through our work are paying continued dividends as we advance agency initiatives such as the Idaho State Historical Museum expansion. Tangible legacies, like collections development and exhibitions continue to serve the public. And, we know, that history builds community; it creates identity, and educates and inspires.

NOTES

1. Our partners included Idaho Public Television, the Department of Parks and Recreation, Idaho Commission on the Arts, Department of Commerce and Tourism, the Idaho Lottery Commission, the Department of Education, and Idaho Commission on Libraries and Idaho associations for museums, cities, and counties, and others.

2. These included: *Essential Idaho: 150 Things That Make the Gem State Unique*, a special exhibition at the Idaho State Historical Museum; *Abraham Lincoln, His Legacy in Idaho*, a permanent exhibition at the Idaho State Archives; *Get Territorial: Idaho at 150*, a traveling exhibition in partnership with the Idaho Humanities Council; *Idaho in 1863*, a commemorative issue of *Idaho Landscapes*; *Ida Visits 150 years of Idaho*, in collaboration with First Lady Lori Otter; *Those Who Served*, a traveling exhibition in collaboration with the Idaho Capitol Commission honoring Idaho veterans; the statewide *Archaeology and Historic Preservation Month*; *Early Governors of Idaho*, a Idaho State Capitol Garden Level Exhibition; the naming of the *Merle Wells Research Center* at the Idaho State Archives; and the naming of the *Lincoln Auditorium* at the Idaho Statehouse.

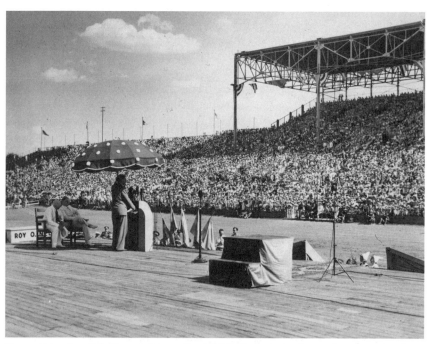

Figure 7.1. Swedish Crown Prince Gustaf Adolf speaks in front of 70,000 people at the New Sweden Tercentenary celebration at the Minnesota State Fair, July 17, 1938. American Swedish Institute.

Chapter 7

Global Histories and Cross-Border Commemoration

Adam Hjorthén

Although this volume was conceived of especially for the American Association of State and Local History, a national organization whose name acknowledges the political boundaries that delineate much of our work, heritage professionals understand that public memory rarely clings to jurisdictional borders. Just as history is a record of "flows and movements across borders," as Adam Hjorthén puts it, so must commemoration reflect the geographic complexity of shared memory. To that end, Hjorthén catalogues several models of cross-border commemoration and provides insight into their various organizational challenges and possibilities. Putting commemoration into global context, we learn, is a matter of ethics. Not only does it encourage wise policy making in the face of an ever-perilous geopolitical milieu, it refocuses our commemorative gaze on individuals whose voices are frequently lost in the hyperbole of national mythologies. Indeed, Hjorthén's central question—"who might think about this history as being 'their own'?"—ought to be a starting point for all commemoration.

—ed.

Commemorations are social events. They are celebrations that demand community participation. But community need not only be local; it can also have a global scope. Many commemorations, in fact, have a broad social range resulting from cooperation across national borders.[1] Commemorations cross national borders more often and in more ways than one might initially think. While some commemorations are the stuff of high-order cooperation between governments, others are organized on local or regional levels. They involve the work of states, counties, municipalities, ethnic associations and religious denominations, and businesses and corporations. As this chapter will show, a global perspective is a great asset for commemorators, but it also presents some potential challenges worth considering.

VARIETIES OF GLOBAL COMMEMORATION

The cross-border commemorations that, perhaps, most readily come to mind are high-profile *nation-to-nation* celebrations. These are events involving both domestic and foreign government agencies as well as the diplomatic missions of foreign states. As a consequence, these events can be described as forums for diplomacy. They commonly serve to historically legitimize friendly international relations. However, the fact that these types of commemorations constitute a form of diplomacy also makes them susceptible to conflict.[2] Commemorations are always to some degree politicized, and this can potentially make them political battlegrounds. A recent example is the 2015 celebration of Victory Day in Moscow, Russia, commemorating the seventieth anniversary of the end of World War II. While previous Victory Days had been attended by heads of states from all countries involved in the war, leaders from the former Allied nations decided to boycott the 2015 celebration. The reason for this decision was Russia's annexation of Crimea and its involvement in the Ukrainian war.[3] Mutual commemorations across national borders can be a statement of historically friendly relations but, as this example demonstrates, breaking a tradition of appearing at joint nation-to-nation commemorations can likewise send a powerful message that signal the end of amity.

Another category is *nation-to-region* (or region-to-nation*)* commemorations. These events are often organized by commissions on either the national or state level, but they are generally performed within more localized contexts. An example is the 400th anniversary of the Jamestown colony in 2007. The commemoration was a massive event initiated by the Virginia General Assembly almost a decade before the start of the actual celebrations. It was supported by the governor and organized by a foundation including members of both the public and private sector. The foundation's explicit objective was for the commemoration to not only have a regional scope but also have national and international significance. A particular focus was placed on tourism and economic development. The commission identified several potential partners in British companies operating in Virginia as well as Virginia-based businesses working in the United Kingdom. These particular partnerships were, of course, legitimized by the fact that the Jamestown colony had been a British settlement. The Virginia commission also established relations with a British committee that was formed to facilitate communications and planning with the United Kingdom. When the commemoration began in 2007, it had a noticeable British presence, most importantly through the participation of a delegation led by Queen Elizabeth II.[4] The Jamestown commemoration was an event that proceeded from a state interest that eventually included national and international cooperation of politicians, state agencies, heritage associations, businesses, and the tourism sector.

A common category of cross-border commemorations, particularly in the United States, can be characterized as *diaspora-to-homeland*. These commemorations concern different levels of cooperation between an ethnic group and various groups in their respective homelands, be it on the national, regional, or local level. It includes cross-border cooperation of different magnitudes, ranging from joint commemorative initiations to a mere invitation of foreign guests to local events. Scholars have regularly interpreted ethnic commemorations in the United States as fundamentally American events, but as many members of ethnic associations can attest to, these celebrations can help establish, renew, or manifest, relations with the lands of their ancestors. An example is the way that Norwegian Americans during the 1930s and 1940s organized several commemorations together with representatives of Norway, celebrating, for example, author Henrik Ibsen and the first Norwegian American settlement in the Fox River Valley in Illinois. These celebrations served to simultaneously promote Norwegian and American nationalisms, and to show Norwegian American support for their old homeland—a factor of great political potency during the Nazi occupation of Norway.[5]

Since at least the early twentieth century, there has also been an increasing involvement of *businesses and corporations* in cross-border commemorations. Quite frequently, businesses piggyback on either of the groups mentioned earlier. Except for practical and organizational reasons, a contributing factor for why businesses are depending on the cooperation of heritage associations, ethnic associations, and state agencies are issues of legitimacy. A commemoration is always launched because of various contemporary interests, but it can be viewed as a problem if the interests at the forefront of the celebrations are overtly commercialized. Although commercial factors might constitute a central aspect of a commemoration, it is often placed in the background of the commemorative programs, being most conspicuously present in the practice of arranging commemorative banquets and luncheons with invited representatives from business and industry. There are also plenty of examples when commercial involvement has facilitated commemorations through joint funding and sponsorships. When, for example, Swedish-American organizations and Sweden in 1948 jointly organized the Swedish Pioneer Centennial, celebrating nineteenth-century pioneer settlements in the Midwest, the commemoration was sponsored by Scandinavian Airlines (SAS) and the Swedish American Line. The two transportation companies thus provided a service to the organizers and could, in turn, use the occasion to promote their businesses on historical grounds.[6]

The distinctions among various kinds of cross-border commemorations are not always clear. In reality, the nation-to-nation, region-to-nation, diaspora-to-homeland, and the involvement of businesses are often mingled. Most commemorations involve some degree of interaction between these different groups and levels. Other groups that participate in cross-border initiatives include religious denominations, federal and state agencies, and various societies and associations. The organizational boundaries in cross-border commemorations are malleable and can very much be shaped according to the needs of the present.

HISTORIES ACROSS NATIONAL BORDERS

Which histories, then, are relevant—or even possible—to commemorate across national borders? Since much of the past is made up of processes that cover large geographical spaces, there are in fact a multitude of such histories. These histories include migration, colonization, wars, slavery, trade, and ideological and cultural exchanges. They can also encompass events such as natural disasters and acts of terrorism. All of these are examples of histories that in one way or another have come about through flows and movements across borders, or that have affected people from different parts of the world.[7]

The fact that some histories have had a strong political, social, or cultural impact on the development of a nation has contributed to their mythological significance in public memory. In the United States, for example, these include the histories of settlement and immigration. What unites the Puritan Pilgrims, the settlers of the Jamestown colony, and the flows of nineteenth- and twentieth-century immigrants from Europe, Asia, and Latin America, is that they all came to North America from another continent. The settlers, pioneers, and immigrants have surely affected the history of the United States. But their legacies have also been important in the countries that they departed. As a consequence, the memories of settlers and immigrants in America have not only been commemorated in America.

There have, for example, been many events similar to the 2007 commemoration of the Jamestown colony. When the short-lived seventeenth-century New Sweden colony (1638–1655) was commemorated in Pennsylvania and Delaware throughout the Delaware River Valley during 2013, it was planned by a joint Swedish-American association and centered on a visit by the King and Queen of Sweden.[8] Conversely, some events that took place outside of

North America have also been commemorated in the United States, with the Holocaust as the most prominent example.[9]

Even such a profound American memory as that associated with the terrorist attacks of September 11, 2001, has not solely been a concern of the United States. There are today numerous 9/11 memorials in Europe, Asia, Australia, and the Middle East, and several countries throughout the world arranged commemorative events at the ten-year anniversary of the attacks. In Paris, a temporary memorial of the Twin Towers was constructed close to the Eiffel Tower, bearing the words "The French Will Never Forget." Indeed, among the victims of the attacks were foreign nationals from ninety-two countries.[10] This attests to the fact that the history of 9/11 also concerns countries other than the United States, and that it thus has the potential to be commemorated across national borders.

WHO'S HISTORY? A QUESTION OF ETHICS

If so much of history concerns movements, flows, and exchanges over large geographical spaces, then to whom does history belong? Does everyone have an equal right to commemorate a certain history? And if several groups appropriate the same history—which rather frequently is the case—then how should we handle conflicting stakes and interests? The ways in which history is represented in commemorations affect how history is envisioned in the present and the future. This is an aspect of commemorations that makes it important not only as a social event but also as a producer of memory and historical knowledge. When commemorations involve several groups, the importance of these processes are further complicated. Suddenly, the reframing of the significance of a certain history becomes dispersed to many groups and societies.

Some histories that cross borders are especially challenging to commemorate, such as slavery, colonial settlement, and wars. These are histories infused by issues of morality, responsibility, and power. Therefore, in commemorations of difficult pasts, and even those that might not seem so difficult, it is important to consider the question: "who might think about this history as being 'their own'?" This is essentially a question of inclusion and exclusion. It encourages commemorative organizers to consider which groups will be involved in the celebration, and on what conditions they are allowed to participate. All groups involved in the planning and performance of commemorations do not have equal cultural, social, educational, or economic capital to participate. These inequalities should not be reasons for dismissing certain groups from being allowed to partake in commemorative organizations. Rather, if a disenfranchised or marginalized group is invited to participate, then it is crucial that representatives of the group can participate in organizing the event on an equal basis as other representatives. As far as possible, all groups participating in the program should have some influence over the commemorative planning.

There have been many cases throughout history where groups that are marginalized in present-day society have not been allowed to take an equal part in organizing commemorations of histories that concern them. In the United States, for instance, excluded groups have often included women, African Americans, and American Indians. Sometimes, the marginalization has been motivated on historical grounds, where the fact that these groups were disenfranchised in the past has been taken as a pretext for marginalizing them today.[11] Here, commemorations of settlement, again, provides an example. Although settler colonial histories certainly concern the American Indian population—past and present—many tribes have not been embraced as equal partners in commemorative planning. American Indians are regularly present in the performance of commemorative programs, but it seems to often be the case that other interests—especially white heritage groups, nonprofits, and businesses—do the bulk of the commemorative planning. This illustrates that inclusion into a cross-border commemoration should be coupled with efforts to reach equal conditions of participation.

ORGANIZING CROSS-BORDER COMMEMORATIONS

Most commemorations are managed in local communities, and local committees often organize even those events that are arranged under the auspices of state or national commissions. This has many practical advantages as these committees have contacts and attachments with the local community in which the event is to take place. The same holds true of commemorations that cross national borders. The fact that a commemoration is the product of cross-border cooperation does not necessarily mean that its organizational body is international or, for that matter, symmetrically distributed between the cooperating nations. On the contrary, the local communities that host core festivities commonly do the majority of the planning. When a commemoration has cross-border qualities, however, it requires that the commissions or committees communicate continuously with the foreign interests. These contacts should ideally be made at an early stage of the process.

A commemoration planned by many different interest groups naturally demands an organization that can facilitate communication and joint planning.

This is sometimes done through the creation of nonprofit associations. The formation of such an organization provides a channel for communication with commissions from abroad. It is vital that organizers, even at this early stage, ask themselves several questions: What groups can be engaged in celebrating or remembering this history? For whom is this history meaningful? How is it meaningful? How can we discuss or represent these dimensions in our commemoration? These questions are particularly important when organizing commemorations across borders, because they prioritize historical thinking over the social, political, and commercial concerns that can quickly seep into planning discussions. Their answers should provide the guidelines for the formation of the commemorative organization.

Cross-border commemorations do not necessarily have to be cofunded or coorganized, but as a general rule they are coperformed. This can include the donation of commemorative plaques or monuments, the coproduction of exhibitions, the publishing of books, or the production and distribution of commemorative memorabilia such as pins, stamps, and coins. The most common way in which a commemoration includes foreign participants is by inviting a person or a delegation from one or several other countries. These contacts have been made easier by the twentieth- and twenty-first-century development of communication technologies. Very few cross-border commemorations are staged without the participation of a foreign representative at some sort of public festival or ceremony. Commemorations in general, but perhaps those that cross borders in particular, regularly place a great importance on figureheads. These people are domestic or foreign dignitaries who function as representatives of the foreign country. They might include high-ranking politicians, diplomats, and heads of state, or representatives of foreign associations or state agencies.

Cross-border commemorations of international or global history has for long been a forgotten category of commemorations. Yet, its popularity has quietly thrived in different parts of the world. In times of changing geopolitical contexts, with nationalism and isolationism currently on the rise, the role and function of commemorations might change in the coming years. There are likely to be more cases similar to the Moscow Victory Day where global commemorations become a display of political conflicts. But as recently showed by President Obama's and Japanese Prime Minister Shinzo Abe's presence at the seventy-fifth anniversary of the attack on Pearl Harbor, celebrations of shared history can also be adopted to promote amity and concord.[12] History can provide a powerful tool of establishing, manifesting, or renewing various relations across national borders, and there is much to be gained by doing so through conscious efforts of organizing cross-border commemorations.

NOTES

1. On transnational or cross-border memory, see Michael Rothberg, *Multidirectional Memory: Remembering the Holocaust in the Age of Decolonization* (Stanford, CA: Stanford University Press, 2009); Udo J. Hebel, ed. *Transnational American Memories* (Berlin: Walter de Gruyter, 2009); Aleida Assmann and Sebastian Conrad, eds. *Memory in a Global Age: Discourses, Practices and Trajectories* (Basingstoke: Palgrave Macmillan, 2010); Julia Creet and Andreas Kitzmann, eds. *Memory and Migration: Multidisciplinary Approaches to Memory Studies* (Toronto: University of Toronto Press, 2011); Chiara De Cesari and Ann Rigney, eds. *Transnational Memory: Circulation, Articulation, Scales* (Berlin: Walter De Gruyter, 2014).

2. Min-Chin Chiang, *Memory Contested, Locality Transformed: Representing Japanese Colonial "Heritage" in Taiwan* (Leiden: Leiden University Press, 2012); Yuki Miyamoto, *Beyond the Mushroom Cloud: Commemoration, Religion, and Responsibility after Hiroshima* (New York: Fordham University Press, 2012).

3. Michael Birnbaum, "One Thing Is Missing from Russia's WWII remembrance—The Allies," *The Washington Post*, May 9, 2015.

4. The official site of America's 400th Anniversary. http://www.jamestown2007.org, accessed March 24, 2016.

5. Daron Olson, *Vikings across the Atlantic: Emigration and the Building of a Greater Norway, 1860–1945* (Minneapolis: University of Minnesota Press, 2013), 159–209; Cf. April R. Schultz, *Ethnicity on Parade: Inventing the Norwegian American Through Celebration* (Amherst: University of Massachusetts Press, 1994); Orm Overland, *Immigrant Minds, American Identities: Making the United States Home, 1870–1930* (Urbana: University of Illinois Press, 2000); Daron W. Olson, *Vikings across the Atlantic: Emigration and the Building of a Greater Norway, 1860–1945* (Minneapolis: University of Minnesota Press, 2013).

6. Adam Hjorthén, *Border-Crossing Commemorations: Entangled Histories of Swedish Settling in America* (Ph.D. diss., Stockholm University, 2015), 181–184.

7. See also, for example, Katie Pickles, *Transnational Outrage: The Death and Commemoration of Edith Cavell* (Basingstoke: Palgrave Macmillan, 2007); J. R. Oldfield, *"Chords of Freedom": Commemoration, Ritual and British Transatlantic Slavery* (Manchester: Manchester University Press, 2007); Reinhart Kössler, "Entangled History and Politics: Negotiating the Past Between Namibia and Germany," *Journal of Contemporary African Studies* 26 (July 2008), 313–339; Henning Melber, "Namibia's Past in the Present: Colonial Genocide and Liberation Struggle in Commemorative Narratives," *South African Historical Journal* 54 (2005), 91–111.

8. New Sweden Alliance, accessed March 24, 2016, http://www.375th.org.

9. Edward T. Linenthal, *Preserving Memory: The Struggle to Create America's Holocaust Museum* (New York: Penguin Books, 1995); Daniel Levy and Natan Sznaider, *The Holocaust and Memory in the Global Age* (Philadelphia, PA: Temple University Press, 2006).

10. Ingrid Gessner, "The Aesthetics of Commemorating 9/11: Towards A Transnational Typology of Memorials," *Journal of Transnational American Studies* 1, no. 6 (2015).

11. Stephen J. Summerhill and John Alexander Williams, *Sinking Columbus: Contested History, Cultural Politics, and Mythmaking during the Quincentenary* (Gainesville: University of Florida Press, 2000); Leslie Witz, *Apartheid's Festival: Contesting South Africa's National Pasts* (Bloomington: Indiana University Press, 2003).

12. Michael S. Schmidt, "Japanese Leader Offers Condolences in Visit to Pearl Harbor," *The New York Times*, December 27, 2016.

Figure 8.1.   1890 portrait of Sir John A. Macdonald, first prime minister of Canada and one of the Fathers of Confederation. Portrait by Pittaway & Jarvis, Library and Archives Canada, C-000686.

Chapter 8

Sir John A. Macdonald and the Problem of Great Men

Jean-Pierre Morin

What is at stake for commemorators who do not, as Adam Hjorthén encourages us, begin by asking "who might think about this history as being 'their own'?" Jean-Pierre Morin provides an answer by probing the challenges of what he terms "Great Man" commemoration. Although Morin's story specifically concerns the calamitous celebration of Canada's foremost great man, Sir John A. Macdonald, its lessons are broadly applicable elsewhere. Most significantly, Morin reminds us that commemoration is always political, and that opting not to confront the politics of public memory is itself a political choice. In this case, the politics in question are national party politics thereby making Macdonald's commemoration a factor in electoral decisions that carry real risks for real people. What is more, we see how the commemorative mingling of Macdonald with the nation itself obscured the historical significance of all the many individuals who contributed to Canada's founding saga. Morin recounts how their ancestors refused to be silenced and, in doing so, offers up a prescient warning to commemorators who fail to accept that their great men may not seem so great to the rest of us.

—ed.

Canadians have been in constant party mode since 2012, commemorating various milestones of their history in the lead up to the 2017 sesquicentennial of the nation's transformation from a grouping of British colonies into the Dominion of Canada.[1] Largely government sponsored, the commemorations have aimed to highlight stages of nation-building, from colony to modern nation. These commemorative moments have also been occasions to recast elements of Canada's history through different perspectives, and have raised concerns about the political "abuse" of history by politicians, especially the government of Prime Minister Stephen Harper. The *Road to 2017* campaign is a case in point, and typifies the use of history as a political trope particularly in its representation of one of the so-called great men of Canadian History: Sir John A. Macdonald.

In Canada, few historical figures have been called a "great man" more often than Macdonald. Described as the architect of modern Canada, Macdonald has been studied and examined since the latter half of the nineteenth century and has served as a benchmark for other political leaders.[2] He was a confederation leader in the 1860s and, most famously, went on to become Canada's first prime minister in 1867. He is occasionally called the "George Washington" of Canada. The *Road to 2017*'s government sponsors intended to present Macdonald as a nation-builder and political visionary. The commemoration did not, however, quite go as planned. Instead, Macdonald's racist policies and legacy of imperialism took center stage, and those hoping to commemorate him as a "great man" were, in some cases, labeled deniers of history and racist themselves for wanting to commemorate such a person. My purpose here is to use the example of Macdonald's commemoration to highlight the challenges inherent in celebrating "great men," and to suggest that long-standing debates about his legacy should have served as a warning to planners from early on.

Born in Scotland in 1815, and having immigrated to Canada as a child, John Alexander Macdonald quickly rose through the colonial political system to become one of its primary figures by the age of 29. A supporter of the British Empire throughout his long political career, he pushed for stronger ties between the colonies to ensure economic prosperity, and also to stave off fears of American expansionism in the wake of the Civil War. Throughout the Confederation debates between 1864 and 1867, Macdonald pushed for a strong centralized national government with clearly defined jurisdictions over the provinces. Upon the ratification of the British North American Act on July 1, 1867, Macdonald became Canada's first prime minister and led an aggressive plan of Western expansion and nation-building, often disregarding the rights and interests of Canada's Indigenous populations. Known for his affable personality, hard drinking, and ruthless political style, Macdonald's legacy has been mixed. He is known as the architect of both Canada's early geographic and economic growth, and its long history of racist immigration policies and forced assimilation of Indigenous peoples.[3]

On January 11, 2015, Prime Minister Stephen Harper marked the bicentennial of Macdonald's birth in Kingston, Ontario, Macdonald's adopted hometown. In a somewhat stereotypical expression of false Canadian modesty, Harper portrayed Canada's first prime minister as "an ordinary man of whom little was expected," but also as a "great man" who "given the opportunity, did extraordinary things."[4] Harper suggested that he remained "a shining example of modesty, hope and success." This was not the first memorialization of Canada's first prime minister. In fact, he is one of the most commemorated individuals in Canadian history with statues, buildings, squares, and roadways bearing his name.[5] The first commemoration began within a few months of his death in 1891, as the House of Commons agreed to fund a statue of his likeness for the grounds of Parliament Hill in Ottawa. By 1895, another four statues had been erected in his honor.[6] This rapid push for commemoration emerged exclusively from within the Macdonald Liberal-Conservative party. By the unveiling of the statues, his political allies had recast him as "the" Father of Confederation, placing him above all other Canadian political figures of the time, and even on par with British heroes like the Duke of Wellington and Lord Horatio Nelson.[7]

Despite all of this, Macdonald's legacy was divisive from the start and he never became a unifying symbol in Canada. Political leaders either distanced themselves from him if they were of the Liberal Party, or embraced him if they were of the Conservative Party.[8] After the 1890s, no significant efforts to memorialize him occurred until the 1930s when the newly established Bank of Canada issued its first series of bank notes with Macdonald's visage on the $500 note and, by 1969, on the $10 note too.[9] By the 1960s, as Canada grappled with the growing independence movement in Quebec, commemorations of Macdonald became linked to those of his French-Canadian ally, Sir George-Étienne Cartier. Macdonald and Cartier had built an English-French alliance to secure confederation in the 1860s. In 1963, their partnership inspired the naming of the Macdonald-Cartier Bridge between Ontario and Quebec by the government of John Diefenbaker. The government of Brian Mulroney renamed the Ottawa airport in their honor in 1993. Both of these commemorations were sponsored by the Progressive-Conservative Party of Canada, the descendant of Macdonald's Liberal-Conservative Party.

The commemoration of Macdonald during *Road to 2017* largely repeated the nineteenth-century emphasis on his role as a nation-builder and as an "important political figure" in Canada. The buildup started in 2013 with a short press release announcing that in 2015, the annual Sir John A. Macdonald Day—which had been recognized since 2002—would be commemorated more significantly than in previous years.[10] Also, a building was to be renamed in his honor, as was one of the most scenic roadways in Ottawa, the capital city, home already to an airport and a bridge carrying Macdonald's name.[11] Along with these initiatives, funding for commemoration activities would be made available to local commemoration organizations, municipalities and history groups such as Historica Canada, while the Royal Canadian Mint and Canada Post unveiled new coins and stamps to commemorate Macdonald. In their announcements, the concept of Macdonald as a "nation-builder" was front and center. The Mint sought to mark "a historic nation-builder and fierce defender of our values and borders."[12] The *Canada Post* celebrated his "success and character."[13]

In Macdonald's hometown of Kingston, Ontario, a local group of historians, business people, and officials formed the John A. Macdonald Commemoration Committee to bring renewed attention to Macdonald's life, achievements, and legacy.[14] Built on a $500,000 funding grant from the Canadian government, the committee created the *SirJohnA2015.ca* initiative, a "multi-faceted project to raise awareness of the life and legacy of Sir John A. Macdonald, Canada's primary architect and first prime minister." *SirJohnA2015.ca* encompassed a number of events in and around Kingston. There was as an outdoor theater experience combining a walking tour of historical attractions and theatrical performances. A series of rotating exhibits commemorated Macdonald's life and legacy at the municipal library that bears his name. And a "Sir John A" week in January 2015 included book launches, films, a skating party, performances of Macdonald's speeches, and a panel discussion on his legacy.[15]

The "great man" theme was also clearly evident in the activities of Historica Canada, an organization aiming to enhance awareness of Canadian history amongst the general public.[16] Historica Canada created three specific online projects focusing on the life and legacy of Macdonald. The first one, Historica's Canadian Encyclopedia exhibit, *Bicentennial of Sir John A. Macdonald's Birth: The Man who Made Canada*, was very direct in its focus. Macdonald was the "father" of Confederation and, "in the pantheon of Canadian superstars, Sir John Alexander Macdonald's credentials are clear . . . to celebrate the shrewd political operator, and visionary prime minister, who more than anyone else made the modern nation of Canada?"[17] The overall focus of the exhibit is on Macdonald's greatness as a political leader and nation-builder, with light treatment of the more difficult aspects of his legacy such as his treatment of Indigenous peoples or Chinese immigrants.

In a second project, the production of a *Heritage Minute* video, an iconic and beloved medium in Canada, Macdonald is again portrayed as the driving force behind the act of union as well as the one with the vision for a "continental" country stretching from the Atlantic to the Pacific.[18] All other political actors of the period are but bit players to Macdonald's grand vision. Historica Canada's final project builds on the *Heritage Minute* model by inviting young people to create their own *Heritage Minutes* on Macdonald.[19] Nearly seventy student-produced videos were uploaded to Historica Canada's website, and nearly all focused on Macdonald's achievements and successes throughout his life.[20] The overall theme was clear: he was the key to creating the Dominion of Canada, further solidifying the view of Macdonald as "the" father of Confederation with everyone else trailing in his wake.

While these initiatives were creating a tightly focused commemoration of Macdonald's "great" legacy, the historical community, journalists, and Indigenous groups openly questioned the negative and less "great" aspects of his life, politics, and impact on Canadian society. They questioned the politicized nature of his commemoration too. As soon as the plans were announced, Prime Minister Harper was accused of using the government-funded commemoration to draw parallels between his leadership and that of Macdonald, especially as the bicentennial landed in an election year.[21] When Ottawa's scenic roadway was renamed for Macdonald in 2011, for example, the *Globe and Mail* newspaper pointed out that it was "the latest initiative by the Conservative government to rebrand and celebrate Conservative icons," just as other buildings had been renamed for other Conservative party leaders.[22] Political pundits accused the ruling Conservatives of "not simply promoting Canadian History. They're re-branding it" for their own political advantages.[23]

In *The Walrus* magazine, a set of articles openly questioned why Macdonald should, or should not, be commemorated. On the one hand, writer Stephen Marche argued that there was no reason to commemorate Macdonald due to his alcoholism, racism, and imperialist policies, and that he deserved "considered and active contempt."[24] In Marche's eye, Macdonald was the opposite of everything that modern Canada holds dear. He was intolerant, racist, and imperialist, or as he puts it "the father of the country we don't want to be." In his reply to Marche, Macdonald biographer, Richard Gwyn, accused him of playing fast and loose with both historical facts and context. His rebuttal cast Marche's arguments as "straw men" and worked to place the criticism of Macdonald's legacy in a grounded historical context.[25] While he correctly chastised Marche for a weak historical assessment, Gwyn's own views of Macdonald's "great man" status dismissed his subject's racist and imperial policies as natural products of the times in which he lived. Gwyn largely glossed over the modern-day impacts of Macdonald's policies.

While journalists and pundits debated the politics of renaming roads and buildings, the historical community also joined the fray. Historians presented papers at the Canadian Historical Association annual meeting on the impacts of Macdonald's Indigenous policies and on his views on white supremacy.[26] New scholarship appeared, including an edited collection of essays, *Macdonald at 200: New Reflections and Legacies*, which stated that it was "high time—for a new take on John A. Macdonald."[27] While not a complete tear down of his legacy, the different essays showed that the historical community was not ready to embrace the same tone as the government's in commemorating Macdonald's impact on modern Canada. On the pages of *ActiveHistory. ca*, a series of articles in the lead-up to the bicentennial brought renewed attention to aspects of Macdonald's legacy being ignored by the government-led initiative. Articles showed that he was openly criticized and depicted as a political manipulator during his career. Others brought to light many of his racist beliefs and their impact on Canada's policies. One writer wondered why the commemorations only focused on men such as Macdonald and completely ignored the role of women in late-nineteenth-century Canada.[28]

It was among Canada's Indigenous community, however, that the "great man" model received the strongest opposition. As the commemoration neared, an ever greater number of comments questioned why the man who had created the foundation of the policies aimed at destroying Indigenous culture was in anyway being celebrated. Fed by the growing historical research into Macdonald's involvement in the creation of these policies, such as residential schools and other assimilation programs, Indigenous commentators outlined Macdonald's legacy of starvation, forced relocation, and the forced removal of children from their families.[29] They stressed that this was the part of his legacy that needed more attention, not his role in Confederation.[30] As the prime minister compared himself to Macdonald, others made similar use of analogy to highlight the failings of the current government's policies toward Indigenous peoples: "This is the man who strategically starved our Indigenous brothers and sisters out west so he could build a railroad. That's a direct precursor to the way mining and oil companies have poisoned countless reserves, causing cancer, diabetes and untold illnesses all in pursuit of the almighty buck."[31] As the criticism grew in the press, so did displeasure with the commemoration, expressed in vandalism of the Macdonald statue in Kingston, Ontario, as well as in direct threats and acts of vandalism against the leaders of the local commemoration committee.[32]

Back in 2013, the Minister of Canadian Heritage said that the commemoration of Sir John A. Macdonald Day was "one of the important celebrations that are bringing Canadians together as we get closer to Canada's 150th anniversary, in 2017. It is important for us all to remember those who laid the cornerstones for future generations to build upon."[33] In reality, the bicentennial of the birth of Canada's first prime minister exposed conflicting interpretations of Macdonald's legacy, thus the difficulties of commemorating "great men." Ultimately, the planned celebration never became the national event that was to help unite Canadians, but rather remained a local commemoration in Macdonald's hometown. The politicization of his legacy, the downplaying of its undeniable impacts on Indigenous peoples, and the prime minister's attempt to link his government with that of the "Old Chieftain," all doomed the commemoration to accusations of whitewashing and rebranding of Canadian history. Interestingly, in that same year, Canadians rejected Stephen Harper's bid for reelection and his party's nine-year rule came to an end in a crushing political defeat. Although certainly more than Macdonald's commemoration explains Harper's defeat, its failure reminds us that the politics of history's great men linger on—for better or for worse—in our choices about how to remember them today.

NOTES

1. "Events, Celebrations and Commemorations", Government of Canada, https://www.canada.ca/en/services/culture/events-celebrations-commemorations.html , (accessed August 2, 2017).

2. "Sir John A. Macdonald: Architect of Modern Canada," CBC Digital Archives, http://www.cbc.ca/archives/topic/sir-john-a-macdonald-architect-of-modern-canada (accessed on August 1, 2016).

3. J.K. Johnson and Tabitha Marshall, "Sir John A. Macdonald," The Canadian Encyclopaedia, March 31, 2015, http://www.thecanadianencyclopedia.ca/en/article/sir-john-alexander-macdonald (accessed August 1, 2017).

4. Bruce Cheadle, "Stephen Harper celebrates 200th university of Sir John A. Macdonald's birth," January 11, 2015, CBCNews, http://www.cbc.ca/news/politics/stephen-harper-celebrates-200th-anniversary-of-sir-john-a-macdonald-s-birth-1.2897073 (accessed August 5, 2016).

5. Although this in no way compares with his American contemporaries. Abraham Lincoln, for example, has over 200 statues of his likeness alone to Macdonald's nine.

6. These appeared in Hamilton, Ontario in 1893; Toronto, Ontario in 1894; Ottawa, Ontario in 1895; and, Montreal, Quebec in 1895. Yves Y. Pelletier, "Politics, Posturing, and Process in Shaping Macdonald's Public Memory (1891-1911)," in P. Dutil and R. Hall, eds., *Macdonald at 200: New Reflections and Legacies* (Toronto: Dundurn Press, 2014), 360.

7. Macdonald Memorial Committee, *The Proceedings at the Unveiling of the Statue of the Late Sir John Alexander Macdonald in Hamilton on the first day of November, 1893* (Hamilton: Macdonald Memorial Committee, 1893), 12.

8. It should be noted that while there are a number of political parties, two parties have dominated the governance of Canada, both of which have their origins in the political factions established before Confederation in 1867: the Liberal Party and the Conservative Party – which has changed names on a number of occasions, from Liberal-Conservative, to Conservative, to Progressive-Conservative, and back to Conservative Party.

9. "1969-1979: The Scenes of Canada Series," Bank of Canada, http://www.bankofcanadamuseum.ca/complete-bank-note-series/1935-first-series/; and, http://www.bankofcanadamuseum.ca/complete-bank-note-series/1969-1979-scenes-canada-series (accessed August 7, 2016).

10. "Sir John A. Macdonald Day, January 11," Government of Canada, http://canada.pch.gc.ca/eng/1455290457640/1455290639393 (accessed August 2, 2016).

11. "Ottawa River Parkway renamed after Sir John A. Macdonald," CBC News, August 15, 2012, http://www.cbc.ca/news/canada/ottawa/ottawa-river-parkway-renamed-after-sir-john-a-macdonald-1.1131806 (accessed August 4, 2016).

12. "Royal Canadian Mint Strikes Circulation Coin to Celebrate 200th Anniversary of the Birth of Sir John A. Macdonald," Royal Canadian Mint, January 11, 2015, http://www.mint.ca/store/news/news-23800049?cat=News+releases&nId=700002&parentn Id=600004&nodeGroup=About+the+Mint#.V6SpZ-srKUl (accessed August 5, 2016).

13. "Sir John A. Macdonald," Canada Post, January 11, 2015, https://www.canadapost.ca/web/en/blogs/collecting/details.page?article=2015/01/11/sir_john_a_mac donald&cattype=collecting&cat=stamps (accessed August 5, 2016).

14. Jane Taber, "Clock starts ticking on Sir John A. Macdonald bicentennial," The Globe and Mail, January 11, 2011, http://www.theglobeandmail.com/news/politics/ottawa-notebook/clock-starts-ticking-on-sir-john-a-macdonald-bicentennial/article1865500 (accessed August 6, 2016).

15. "Reimagined Production for 2015," SALON Theater Productions, http://www.sirjohna2015.ca/in-sir-john-as-footsteps.html (accessed August 6, 2016); "Sir John A Bicentennial", City of Kingston, https://www.cityofkingston.ca/explore/culture-history/history/sir-john-a/bicentennial (accessed August 2, 2017); and "Macdonald Week January 6-11," http://www.sirjohna2015.ca/uploads/2/5/6/7/25676799/sirjamacdonald2015brochure-finaldec11.pdf (accessed August 6, 2016).

16. "About", Historica Canada, https://www.historicacanada.ca/about , accessed August 2, 2017.

17. "Bicentennial of Sir John A. Macdonald's Birth", The Canadian Encyclopedia, http://www.thecanadianencyclopedia.ca/en/exhibit/bicentennial-of-sir-john-a-macdonalds-birth/ accessed August 2, 2017.

18. Canadian Heritage Minutes are a series of 60-second videos, first created in 1991, focusing on various aspects of Canadian history and were designed to be distributed to schools and to play as a type of public service announcement during television breaks. There are currently 88 Heritage Minutes available for viewing on the Historica Canada website and on YouTube at https://www.historicacanada.ca/content/heritage-minutes/agnes-macphail (accessed August 8, 2016); and, http://www.gotaminute.ca/ (accessed August 9, 2016).

19. "Stories of Sir John A., Student Resources," Historica Canada, http://storiesofsirjohna.ca/#student-resources (accessed August 9, 2016).

20. "Stories of Sir John A., Contest Gallery," Historica Canada, http://storiesofsirjohna.ca/gallery/ (accessed August 9, 2016).

21. Thomas Peace, "Canadians and their Pasts on the Road to Confederation," ActiveHistory.ca, January 20, 2014, http://activehistory.ca/2014/01/canadians-and-their-pasts-on-the-road-to-2017 (accessed August 4, 2016).

22. Omair Quadri, "Sir John A. gets a new road as Tories paint Ottawa blue," The Globe and Mail, August 15, 2012, http://www.theglobeandmail.com/news/politics/sir-john-a-gets-a-new-road-as-tories-paint-ottawa-blue/article4482551 (accessed August 5, 2016).

23. Scott Reid, "On Political Parkways", Ottawa Citizen, August 18, 2012. http://www.pressreader.com/canada/ottawa-citizen/20120818/281535108147966 (accessed August 2, 2017).

24. Stephen Marche, "Old Macdonald" https://thewalrus.ca/old-macdonald/ (accessed August 2, 2017).

25. Richard Gwyn, "Canada's First Scapegoat", https://thewalrus.ca/canadas-first-scapegoat/ (accessed August 2, 2017).

26. Donald Smith and Allan Sherwin, "John A. Macdonald's Relationship with Aboriginal Peoples", Canadian Historical Association, Annual Meeting, 2014; Timothy Stanley, "The Presentism of Racist Denial: Sir John A Macdonald, White Supremacy and the Cultural Politics of Historical Memory", Canadian Historical Association, Annual Meeting, 2013.

27. Patrice Dutil and Roger Hall, "Introduction: a Macdonald for our Times", in P. Dutil and R. Hall, eds., *Macdonald at 200: New Reflections and Legacies* (Toronto: Dundurn Press, 2014), 13.

28. Thomas Peace, "Old Chieftain or Old Charlatan? Assessing Sir John's Complex Legacy through Political Cartoons," ActiveHistory.ca, January 6, 2015, http://activehistory.ca/2015/01/old-chieftain-or-old-charlatan-assessing-sir-johns-complex-legacy-through-political-cartoons (accessed August 7, 2016); Thomas J. Stanley, "John A. Macdonald's Aryan Canada: Aboriginal Genocide and Chinese Exclusion," Active History.ca, January 7, 2015, http://activehistory.ca/2015/01/john-a-macdonalds-aryan-canada-aboriginal-genocide-and-chinese-exclusion (accessed August 7, 2016); Christa Zeller Thomas, "Birthing a Dominion," ActiveHistory.ca, January 8, 2015, http://activehistory.ca/2015/01/birthing-a-dominion (accessed August 7, 2016).

29. Such as James Daschuk, *Clearing of the Plains* (Regina: University of Regina Press, 2014).

30. Dough Cuthand, "Sir John A. Macdonald's birthday cause for reflection, not celebration for First Nations," CBCNews, January 11, 2015, http://www.cbc.ca/news/aboriginal/sir-john-a-macdonald-s-birthday-cause-for-reflection-not-celebration-for-first-nations-1.2895872 (accessed August 9, 2016).

31. Anonymous contributor, "Let's celebrate surviving Sir John A. Macdonald," Two Row Times, January 20, 2015, https://tworowtimes.com/opinion/lets-celebrate-surviving-sir-john-macdonald (accessed August 9, 2016).

32. "Vandals target organizer of Sir John A. Macdonald tribute in Kingston," The Globe and Mail, January 11, 2016, http://www.theglobeandmail.com/news/national/vandals-target-organizer-of-sir-john-a-macdonald-tribute-in-kingston-ont/article28116685 (accessed August 9, 2016).

33. Hon. James Moore, Minister of Canadian Heritage https://www.canada.ca/en/news/archive/2013/01/statement-honourable-james-moore-minister-canadian-heritage-official-languages-sir-john-macdonald-day.html (accessed August 2, 2017).

Figure 9.1.   Members of the Boston Area Lesbian and Gay History Project, June 1980 in front of Trinity Church in Copley Square at the annual Boston Pride March and Rally. Courtesy of The History Project, Boston, Massachusetts.

Chapter 9

Gay Is Good

Commemorating LGBTQ History

Kenneth C. Turino

As this volume has shown, broadening commemoration to include all varieties of people—as subjects and participants—must be a priority for heritage organizations concerned to celebrate the past. And yet, as it has been practiced, commemoration tends to enshrine stereotypes: the solider, the victim, the hero, the pioneer. How do we break the mold? How do we make room in our historical imagination for more and more kinds of representative actors? Kenneth C. Turino offers one perspective in this, the first of several essays to consider emergent themes in American commemorative practice. Turino senses a sea change in how Americans recognize lesbian, gay, bisexual, transsexual, and queer (LGBTQ) history. It is a trend, he shows us, with a history of its own. And what that history suggests is that now is the time to encourage a fuller and more capacious engagement with LGBTQ history throughout the nation's heritage landscape. It would be a mistake, Turino suggests, to conceive of LGBTQ history as merely a record of violence and resistance. Rather commemoration provides an opportunity to celebrate the remarkable diversity of ordinary lives and, in doing so, bind us all together against the wages of hate and inequality.

—ed.

While visiting Philadelphia in 2012 to see the NPS's recently opened President's House monument, I happened to be standing across the street from Independence Hall and the Liberty Bell Center when I noticed a different kind of historical marker. The subject of this marker was not typical insomuch as it did not describe a historic battle or incident or person of note. Instead, this marker commemorated annual gay rights demonstrations led by gay activists on Independence Day from 1965 to 1969, as the sign states, "for gay and lesbian equality." It was dedicated in 2005 to the fortieth anniversary of the first demonstration. It is interesting to note that the marker commemorates an annual event that was a precursor to the first Gay Pride parades. What really surprised me, though, was that there was a marker at all honoring LGBTQ history. Standing there, I couldn't help but wonder how we got to the point where LGBTQ history is noted on historical markers.

That it is begs a whole host of important questions for heritage professionals and would-be commemorators: Has LGBTQ history made its way into the mainstream? Do we commemorate LGBTQ history and events differently from other history and events? How can we as public historians encourage historic site managers to incorporate and commemorate LGBTQ history at their properties? In my work as a gay public historian in the last two decades, I have seen slow but steady progress being made in interpreting diverse stories at historic sites, with more and more acknowledging previously hidden histories. These changes in the history field, including the growing albeit slower acceptance of LGBTQ history, run parallel to and reflect national trends. In this chapter, I examine how LGBTQ history has been commemorated, and how public historians in national, state, and local agencies and museums can play a role in continuing this.

Most historians agree that the Stonewall riots—spontaneous, violent demonstrations by members of the gay community against a police raid that took place in the early morning of June 28, 1969, at the Stonewall Inn in New York City's Greenwich Village—served as a galvanizing event, spurring on the gay liberation movement and the modern fight for LGBTQ rights. The battle for LGBTQ rights had been going on for decades, however, and as Susan Ferentinos writes, "Stonewall was part of a much larger trajectory in which LGBT people became increasingly organized and eventually radicalized in their efforts to improve the circumstances of their lives."[1] One example of these earlier efforts was the Society for Human Rights, founded by Henry Gerber in Chicago in 1924, the first gay rights organization in America. But up until then Stonewall progress was slow. After the Stonewall riots, gays and lesbians appeared to become a much more cohesive community. Within the year, gay activist organizations formed in Chicago, New York, Boston, and other major cities across the United States, and these continued to grow and spread around the country.

LGBTQ commemoration, for the most part, began with Gay Pride marches. The first marches took place on June 28, 1970, in New York City, Los Angeles, San Francisco, and Chicago and marked the anniversary of the Stonewall riots. Acts of commemoration in the LGBTQ community have been, from the beginning, distinctly political, in contrast to more recent efforts, which tend to focus more on monuments and historic markers. And yet, as we have seen throughout this volume, all commemoration is political. Militancy, marches, and demonstrations characterized how the gay community and other movements of the time brought awareness of their cause to the general public. The Stonewall riots and the Gay Pride marches of the late 1960s and 1970s happened at a time of great cultural change in the United States, with opposition to the Vietnam War growing and a focus on social movements for justice, especially in terms of race, women's rights, and gay liberation. The Gay Pride marches, which could be confrontational, were used both to commemorate Stonewall and as platforms to advocate for equal rights. In addition, they were and still are a celebration of LGBTQ community. The marches and demonstrations were very much of their time. As Dell Upton writes, these commemorations "say more about the people, times and places of their creation than they do about the people, times and places they honor."[2]

The LGBTQ community continued to use marches and other strategies through the 1970s and 1980s. Organizations such as the AIDS Coalition to Unleash Power (ACT UP), an advocacy group, successfully demonstrated and lobbied for legislation, medical research, treatment, and policies to end the AIDS pandemic. Events such as the October 1979 National March on Washington for Lesbian and Gay Rights and another National March on Washington in October 1987, this one to demand that President Ronald Reagan address the AIDS crisis, also garnered attention. It was during the latter march that the AIDS Memorial Quilt was first displayed at the National Mall. An estimated half a million people viewed the Quilt, which covered a space larger than a football field.

The mission of the creators of the AIDS Memorial Quilt, who formed an organization called the NAMES Project Foundation in 1987 in San Francisco, was to "provide a creative means for remembrance and healing" as well as to raise funds to support AIDS service organizations. According to the NAMES Project Foundation website, the Quilt "is a powerful visual reminder of the devastating effect of the AIDS pandemic. More than 48,000 individual 3–6-foot memorial panels—mostly commemorating the life of someone who has died of AIDS—have been sewn together by friends, lovers and family members." The Quilt was displayed in twenty cities in 1988, returned to Washington, and had a second national tour in 1989. The last public display of the entire Quilt was at the National Mall in 1996. The NAMES Project Foundation remains active today, continuing its goals of AIDS awareness and public education for AIDS prevention as well as caring for and exhibiting the Quilt.[3]

Today, LGBTQ Pride marches and events are held annually in June to mark the Stonewall riots, and these marches are still very much a part of LGBTQ commemoration. In 2016, San Francisco's Castro neighborhood will host the thirty-eighth annual anniversary march to honor Harvey Milk, a member of the city's Board of Supervisors, and Mayor George Moscone, both assassinated by Dan White, a former city supervisor. The annual candlelit march includes a flower shrine at Harvey Milk Plaza in remembrance of Milk and Moscone.

Since the 1980s, the LGBTQ rights movement has suffered tremendous setbacks and has made significant strides forward. The setbacks included President Bill Clinton signing the Defense of Marriage Act prohibiting federal recognition of same-sex marriages in 1996. But the movement has also made great advances. In 2004, Massachusetts became the first state to allow same-sex marriage. The U.S. Supreme Court ruled in 2015 that all Americans, no matter their gender or sexual orientation, are free to marry. With all these social and political changes, has the more militant stance for LGBTQ rights reflected in its commemorations taken a back seat as the LGBTQ community has received more acceptance? As the chant "We're Here, We're Queer, Get Used to it" demanded, have we gotten used to it?[4] Are gay culture and the quest for equal rights becoming more mainstreamed? It certainly is prevalent in popular culture with LGBTQ characters (and not just stereotypes) regularly featured on television and in films. The fact that more and more traditional forms of commemorating LGBTQ life are popping up seems to point to the general acceptance of LGBTQ culture and equal rights.

LGBTQ history is becoming more visible to the public and openly discussed, as we saw at the outset, in historical markers. In October 2009, Ohio honored Natalie Barney, a lesbian writer and literary patron who was born in Dayton, with a historical marker noting her sexual orientation. In addition to Philadelphia's Gay Rights Demonstrations historical marker, in 2011, the city erected a marker to Giovanni's Room, a bookstore founded in 1973 that "provided resources to those working to gain legal rights for LGBT people." A memorial plaque also appears at the New Orleans site of the UpStairs Lounge. It was there on Sunday, June 24, 1973, the final day of Pride Weekend, that a social gathering at the pro-LGBT Protestant Metropolitan Community Church was attacked by arson, resulting in thirty-two deaths.[5]

Another traditional way of memorializing is through sculpture. One of the earliest LGBTQ sculptures, *Gay Liberation* by George Segal, was erected by the City of New York in 1992 to commemorate the Stonewall riots. A more recent example of sculpture as memorial is Puerto Rico's first LGBTQ monument, designed by Alberto de la Cruz and dedicated to the forty-nine victims (mainly Latino men and women) of the Pulse nightclub massacre in Orlando, Florida. This massacre, one of the largest mass shootings in the United States, is in line with contemporary modes of mourning that, as memory scholar Erika Doss puts it, create "archives of public affect."[6] The grieving for the victims was expressed with temporary memorials of flowers, crosses, photographs of the victims, and mementos in Orlando and in cities across the country. The City of Orlando has announced plans for a permanent memorial.

Perhaps the most memorialized gay individual is activist and politician Harvey Milk, for whom a statue was dedicated in San Francisco City Hall in May 2008 to commemorate his service to the city. Milk, the subject of a major Hollywood biographical film titled *Milk* and released in 2008, was also honored in May 2014 with a postage stamp at a White House ceremony and with a special dedication ceremony in San Francisco that same month. In August 2016, the Navy announced that it would commemorate Milk's life by naming a new 677-foot fleet oiler the USNS *Harvey Milk*, making it the first Navy ship to be named after a member of the LGBTQ community. As the LGBTQ community has grown in acceptance, it has also grown in power and exerted its influence. These commemorations are examples of what Doss sees as "grounded in a vastly expanded US demographic and heightened expectations of rights and representation among the nation's increasing diverse publics."[7]

Libraries, and to an increasing extent mainstream history museums, have begun commemorating LGBTQ life or become sites of commemorating LGBTQ life through temporary exhibitions. Early instances include the landmark exhibitions *Becoming Visible: The Legacy of Stonewall*, which opened at the New York Public Library in June 1994, and *Public Faces/Private Lives*, produced by The History Project and opened in 1996 at the Boston Public Library.[8] Recent exhibitions include *Out in Chicago* at the Chicago History Museum, which opened in May 2011, and *Revealing Queer*, which opened in February 2014 at the Museum of History and Industry in Seattle. Equally important, mainstream museums are incorporating this history in their permanent overview exhibitions, as in the case of the Museum of History and Industry in Seattle and *True Northwest: The Seattle Journey*. It was only in 2011 that Russell Lewis wrote "mainstream history museums have without almost no exception, excluded lesbian, gay, bisexual, and transgender communities from the local state, regional, and national narratives they present to the public in their exhibitions."[9] This too, seems to be changing. Even whole museum's dedicated to LGBTQ history and to telling this community's story have opened. These include the Stonewall National Museum & Archives in the Ft. Lauderdale Branch Library and ArtServe building in Fort Lauderdale, and the LGBT Historical Society in San Francisco. Both of these museums seek to reach out to not just the LGBTQ community but to more general audiences as well.

Other indications of acceptance for the LGBTQ community and its history can be seen in the fact that the NPS, which is "the major institutional body charged with shaping national identity through its management of America's national parks, memorials, monuments, and historic sites," now acknowledges, interprets, and commemorates LGBTQ history.[10] On June 24, 2016, the site of the Stonewall riots in Greenwich Village was recognized as the first official NPS unit dedicated to telling the story of LGBTQ Americans. The new Stonewall National Monument will contain approximately 7.7 acres of land, including Christopher Park, the Stonewall Inn, and the surrounding streets and sidewalks that were the site of the riots. The Stonewall Monument is a milestone in the recognition of LGBTQ history on the national level, and appears to be only the beginning of much broader commemoration. The NPS has launched several theme studies that, in Director Jon Jarvis's words, "explore ways that we can increase recognition of underrepresented groups in the National Park System."[11] These include an LGBTQ theme study and the LGBTQ Heritage Initiative, which has been rolled into the broader NPS project of "Telling All Americans' Stories." According to Megan Springate, prime consultant to the LGBTQ Heritage Initiative, "we're not a 'special project' anymore; we're part of the overall fabric of the NPS." The recognition and commemoration of these sites is yet another indication of the great advances the LGBTQ community has made in mainstream society.[12]

Besides historical markers and identifying sites for National Historic Landmarks and the National Register of Historic Places, what else can public historians and museum professionals do to promote and commemorate LGBTQ history? Many organizations like the History Project in Boston are offering walking tours of neighborhoods or are developing self-guided walking tours like the Rainbow History Project in Washington, D.C. The NPS has web pages with suggestions on how the public can get involved with LGBTQ history including memorialization and commemoration. Tips include creating salons to discuss LGBTQ history, lobbying museums for exhibitions, mapping sites associated with LGBTQ history, and collecting documents, artifacts and oral histories.[13] Much of what the NPS is advocating for are traditional ways of presenting and commemorating history. Is this enough?

One of the most creative and active groups promoting the history of the LGBTQ community is the New York City LGBT Historic Sites Project, which documents and actively lobbies for sites throughout the city. A goal of the project is to recognize LGBTQ historic sites for their potential to positively impact LGBTQ youth. In addition to standard types of programs such as lectures and tours, in celebration of LGBT Pride Month in June 2016, the group placed rainbow flags at the gravesites of well-known LGBTQ figures at historic Woodlawn Cemetery in the Bronx and at Green-Wood Cemetery in Brooklyn.[14] According to Andrew S. Dolkart, codirector of the NYC LGBT Historic Sites Project and a historic preservation professor at Columbia University, "often grave sites are the one tangible memorial to LGBT men and women who contributed immeasurably to New York City and to the nation."

Commemorative activities in the LGBTQ community, from the first Pride marches to more recent memorials, regularly commemorate violent or tragic events. These include the Stonewall Riots, the assassination of Harvey Milk, the murder of Matthew Shepard, and the shootings at the Pulse nightclub in Orlando.[15] Americans seem to have embraced facets of gay culture, but LGBTQ commemoration must celebrate that culture as well. The fact that the NPS recognizes sites that are not only overtly political—like the Cherry Grove Community House and Theater on Fire Island in New York, what the NPS calls "America's First Gay and Lesbian Town"—is an important step forward. And yet, while the LGBTQ movement has gained acceptance, much like the civil rights movement, the battle is unfortunately not over. LGBTQ people still face violence, hate crimes, and discrimination. Even as I write, the U.S. Supreme Court is considering the case of Gavin Grimm, a high school senior in Gloucester, Virginia. Grimm, who identifies as male though he was born female, is not allowed to use his school's boys' restrooms. His case challenges the school's policy barring him from using the bathroom of his choice. At the same time, the city of Salem, Massachusetts, is reacting force-fully against the hate crime of the detonation of an explosive placed inside a news box for the LGBTQ newspaper, *The Rainbow Times*.

So, to go back to the slogan, "We're Here, We're Queer, Get Used to It," we certainly are here and while many Americans have gotten used to it, clearly there is still a long way to go. If public historians and museum staff want to continue to commemorate LGBTQ history while acknowledging the continued battle, their programs, like many of the best offered at our historic sites, need to be more active and participatory. In keeping with the political aspect of LGBTQ memorialization, we need to look for ways that will keep that part of our history alive.

NOTES

1. Susan Ferentinos, *Interpreting LGBT History at Museums and Historic Sites* (Lanham, MD: Rowman & Littlefield Publishers, 2014), 75.
2. Dell Upton, "Why Do Contemporary Monuments Talk So Much?," in David Gobel and Daves Rossell, eds. *Commemoration in America: Essays on Monuments, Memorialization, and Memory* (Charlottesville and London: University of Virginia Press, 2013), 20.
3. The NAMES Project Foundation, http://www.aidsquilt.org/.
4. Slogan coined by gay rights activist Frank Kameny and used by gay rights pro-ponents following the Stonewall riots to respond to the widely held view that being gay was wrong and shameful.
5. For an overview of these instances and others, see Kenneth C. Turino and Susan Ferentinos, "Entering the Mainstream, Interpreting LGBT History," *History News* 67:4 (Autumn 2012), 21–25.
6. Erika Doss, *Memorial Mania: Public Feeling in America* (Chicago, IL; and London: The University of Chicago Press, 2010), 13.
7. Doss, *Memorial Mania*, 19.
8. The exhibit traveled throughout Massachusetts and became the basis for a book. See the History Project, *Improper Bostonians: Lesbian and Gay History from the Puritans to Playland* (Boston, MA: Beacon Press, 1999).

9. Pg. vii. Out in Chicago, LGBT history at the Crossroads. Chicago History Museum, Jill Austin and Jennifer Frier editors Chicago History Museum, 2011.

10. Doss, *Memorial Mania*, 55.

11. Jarvis cited at http://transcripts.castingwords.com/2Oo/180371.htm.

12. Since May 2014, when the NPS began the LGBTQ theme study, many LGBTQ sites were designated National Historic Landmarks or listed on the National Register of Historic Places. These include sites associated with activists such as the Dr. Franklin E. Kameny Residence in Washington, DC (November 2, 2011) and the Henry Gerber House in Chicago,Ill., (June 9, 2015). Also, properties used by the LGBTQ community for socializing, such as Julius's Bar in New York, (April 20, 2016) and Cherry Grove Community House & Theater in Cherry Grove, New York (June 4, 2014). Sites for meetings and LGBTQ organization meeting places such as the Furies Collective house in Washington, D.C. (May 5, 2016), and Edificio Comunidad de Orgullo Gay de Puerto Rico (known as Casa Orguillo, or Pride House) in San Juan, Puerto Rico (May 5, 2016). When complete, the study will be available at https://www.nps.gov/subjects/tellingallamericansstories/lgbtqthemestudy.htm.

13. https://www.nps.gov/heritageinitiatives/LGBThistory/involved.html

14. Gravesites flagged included suffragists Carrie Chapman Catt and Mary Garrett Hay, Harlem Renaissance luminary Countee Cullen, playwrights Clyde Fitch and Roi Cooper Megrue, sculptor Malvina Hoffman and Emma Stebbins, muralist Violet Oakley, illustrator JC Leyendecker, photographer George Platt Lynes, composers Leonard Bernstein and Louis Moreau, musical theater lyricist Fred Ebb, vaudeville star and female impersonator Bert Savoy, as well as prominent attorney John Sterling, psychiatrist and gay rights activist Richard Isay, singer/songwriter and actor Paul Jabara, sculptor.

15. Shepard is commemorated by a memorial bench on the campus of the University of Wyoming.

Figure 10.1.   Interpreters at the Ephrata Cloister in Lancaster County, Pennsylvania, dress in the distinctive religious garb of the site's original, eighteenth-century inhabitants. Craig A. Benner/Ephrata Cloister.

Chapter 10

Sacred Subjects

Religion and Commemoration in America

Devin C. Manzullo-Thomas

Memory and faith are everywhere entangled in the long history of American commemorative practice. That they are should come as no surprise. Tammy Gordon hints at the connection in her likening of exhibits to funerals. And we learned from William Walker that commemorative festivals repackage ancient rituals in secular guise. But is there more here than just casual resemblance? Devin C. Manzullo-Thomas shows us that there is and that resonances among communities of memory and communities of faith provide fascinating opportunities for commemorative programming. "Public memory," Manzullo-Thomas points out, "is often formed in the crucible of religious emotion." And because the nation's history is distinguished by conflict, collisions, and confluences among myriad faith groups, even our most secular expressions of shared memory are run through with religiosity. Sifting through these fascinating entanglements is one step toward identifying ways that commemorative planning can engage audiences across the spectrum of belief. It is also an essential bulwark in our age of hyper partisanship against the politicians and pundits who would have us believe that one way of believing is more legitimate than another.

—ed.

Religion saturates the American commemorative landscape. Historical markers adorn church buildings and synagogues across the country. Congregations celebrate anniversaries with memorabilia displays, historical reenactments, heritage pageants, and other festivities. Denominational archives stage exhibits using artifacts and documents drawn from their collections; communities erect monuments to religious figures in public spaces; and devotees rescue, restore, and preserve the birthplaces of their leaders. Meanwhile, many seemingly secular sites of national memory—battlefields, birthplaces, and museums—cast their significance in spiritual language, referring to themselves as "sacred sites" to which visitors make regular pilgrimages. And a few such sites even attempt to interpret the historical significance of American religions. In these ways and many others, as the historian Christopher Cantwell has argued, "the institutions, experiences, and ideas marked as religious both inform and animate America's relationship with its past."[1]

This chapter explores the informing and animating force of commemoration within America's religious communities as well as the presence of religious themes in the discourse of public memory. It begins with a brief and by no means comprehensive historical survey of religious commemoration in America. It then offers a paradigm for understanding the different ways that religion gets commemorated in America, and concludes with some suggestions regarding key issues that would-be commemorators should keep in mind.

A BRIEF HISTORY OF COMMEMORATION
AND RELIGION IN AMERICA

The public use of collective memory among religious adherents in America began even before the nation's founding. Historical commemoration at this time provided a way for religious groups to lay claim to their local communities, and a means by which to inculcate religious virtues in present and future generations. In 1741, for instance, nonagenarian New Englander and Puritan elder Thomas Faunce launched a public and highly emotional campaign to preserve the rock in Plymouth Harbor where Puritan "forefathers" had reportedly stepped onto the New World.[2] Later, in the early nineteenth century, as swelling civic pride prompted Americans to collect old documents, preserve aging buildings, and write narratives of local communities, religious Americans adapted civic practices of commemoration for their own purposes.[3] For instance, the nation's oldest denominations—the Congregationalists and Presbyterians—developed a format for marking church anniversaries through sermonic "historical discourses," and published congregational histories.

These products reflected the civic- and community-oriented purposes of local history but also emphasized a distinct, Protestant view of history as a teacher of moral and theological lessons. As one Presbyterian minister declared, "The history of God's dealings with the children of men is full of instruction."[4] Beyond the oral and written record, congregations also celebrated with informal picnics, the recitation of homemade poems and hymns, and displays of "sacred objects" such as congregational charters, Bibles, or preserved pieces of historic church buildings.[5] By the mid-nineteenth century, these denominations also established centralized archival repositories for the

deposition of official church materials, a process that paralleled the formation of state and local historical societies.[6] In these ways and others, religious
communities used the past to address present-day concerns: to strengthen
collective identity, to nurture civic pride, to improve the nation's moral character, and to create connections between human and the divine.

Yet by the last quarter of the nineteenth century, America's religious
landscape had shifted dramatically. The established denominations lost their
demographic prominence to younger groups such as the Methodists and
Baptists. New religious movements, including Mormonism, emerged and
grew rapidly. And waves of immigration from Eastern Europe brought to
America's shores more Catholics and Jews than ever before.[7] Like the established churches, America's new religious groups used history to constitute
their collective identity. These groups also deployed historical performance,
monument building, and the preservation of sacred sites to claim their rights
of citizenship and to assert the Americanness of their particular religious
tradition.

For instance, beginning in the late nineteenth century, American Jews produced and participated in a variety of commemorative activities—parades,
pageants, and popular literature, among others—designed to assimilate new
immigrants to American democratic values while also bolstering collective identity and group pride. While Jews yet lacked the cultural power to
affirm their communities through more conventional commemorative forms,
such as museums, the historian Beth Wenger has observed that well into the
twentieth century selected practices of commemoration "both eased Jewish
adjustment to American life and created a distinct ethnic history compatible
with American ideals."[8] During the same period, American Mormons also
deployed commemorative activities to bolster collective identity and make
claims of citizenship. Beginning in the 1890s, the Church of Jesus Christ of
Latter-Day Saints purchased a series of properties, including the birthplace
of church founder Joseph Smith, and transformed them into public historical
sites. Occurring in tandem with the church's turn away from polygamy and
toward the quest for social respectability, this burst of historical commemoration enabled church members simultaneously to forget aspects of a communal
past, to give legitimacy to church history and doctrine, and to link a version
of the Mormon story to America's national civic narratives.[9] According to the
historian Keith A. Erekson, Mormons used Smith's birthplace site to forge
the image of their founder as "America's prophet" and to "emphasize the
Americanness of Mormonism," while simultaneously downplaying aspects
of the tradition's early history.[10]

Thus, by the mid-twentieth century, America's religious communities had
made their mark on the nation's commemorative landscape. At the same time,
many Americans—religious and nonreligious alike—increasingly employed

the language of spiritual transcendence to describe seemingly secular sites of public memory. For instance, an 1886 guidebook to the Civil War battlefield in Gettysburg, Pennsylvania, described the site as "the most consecrated ground this world contains." A half-century later, another commentator called the battlefield at Little Bighorn, in Montana, "sacred ground" and compared it to the biblical site of Christ's crucifixion.[11] Such evocations served to inspire patriotic fervor and civic pride, a critical function of many national historical sites in the late nineteenth and early twentieth centuries.[12] The language also reflected the historic dominance of Protestant Christian rhetoric in many areas of American life, including popular history-making. But such language has persisted well into the supposedly secular twentieth and twenty-first centuries, as battlefields, birthplaces, and other sites continue to promote themselves using sacralized expressions. Yet in these spaces, religion functions primarily as a metaphor; state- and federally run sites of public memory tend to dismiss religious ideas or institutions as markers of historical legitimacy or significance. Nevertheless, these examples underscore the myriad ways in which a sense of the numinous continues to condition Americans' connections to the past.

MODES OF RELIGIOUS COMMEMORATION

For the last thirty or so years, American religious commemoration typically has reflected one of two modes. The first might be termed "private history made public."[13] In this mode, religious people develop commemorative projects primarily for other religious people. The goal is to create a shared sense of the past, or to generate tourist dollars, or both. Nevertheless, the projects themselves—performances, exhibitions, memorializations, historic site management, and the like—often occur in spaces open to (and sometimes geared toward) broader public consumption. Congregational anniversary celebrations are perhaps the most obvious example of this mode.[14] Denomination- or congregation-run archives and museums exhibit similar characteristics.[15] Moreover, when speaking specifically to outsiders, some commemorative projects in this mode adopt an evangelistic tone, deploying history as a tool for proselytizing visitors to join the faith.[16]

These qualities demonstrate that private-made-public historical projects, like other community-led history-making, rely upon and reflect the motivations of community members. They often draw more on local community knowledge and goals than on the knowledge and goals of public history professionals. As the historian Tammy Gordon has observed, creators of community commemorations "are quite candid about not adhering to the historical profession's objectivity values."[17] Gordon describes the Billy Sunday Visitors Center in Winona Lake, Indiana, as a vivid illustration of these dynamics. Housed inside the tabernacle where on Sunday, an early twentieth-century American evangelical preacher hosted many revival services, the museum features expertly designed exhibits intended for an evangelical Christian audience already familiar and in agreement with the purposes of Sunday's evangelistic work. Gordon describes how the exhibits rely "on visitors' adherence to the goals of evangelism . . . [and make] consistent connections to the positive value of Sunday's work."[18] On a few occasions the exhibits observe the professional practice of acknowledging opposing views and voices; however, the museum's overall curatorial voice marginalizes those perspectives by "privileging an interpretation that serves evangelical goals," according to Gordon.[19] As the Sunday Visitors Center underscores, commemorative projects in the private-made-public mode often serve diverse publics, even though the typical target audience is community insiders who share commemorators' general perspectives and support their purposes.

The second mode of religious commemoration might be termed "public history made private." In this mode, entities including state and federal historical agencies, as well as nonprofit organizations not run by religious groups, commemorate and interpret America's religious past for a broad audience. These projects go beyond references to civic "sacredness" or tourist pilgrimages, to engage actual religious ideas, institutions, experiences, or communities.

Despite the sometimes intimate and private nature of the subject matter, these projects are carried out principally by public history professionals who adhere to professional standards. However, examples of this mode are few. Many public history practitioners and educators hesitate to incorporate religion into public projects. Cantwell postulates that these professionals fear reviving the "History Wars" of the 1980s and 1990s, or that they feel uncomfortable making the supernatural, moral, or explicitly theological claims about the past that religious communities tend to expect.[20] Others point to the reductive criteria employed by public agencies in assessing the historical value of a religious site selected for preservation and commemoration. The National Register of Historic Places, for instance, limits the selection of a religious site to its quantifiable qualities—"architectural or artistic distinction or historical importance"—even though religious communities typically view such sites as possessing spiritual or communal value.[21] For these reasons and others, religion often gets left out of publicly sanctioned commemorative activities.

Nevertheless, examples do exist. The Ephrata Cloister—nestled in the rolling farmland of Lancaster County, Pennsylvania, and surrounded by the region's Amish and Mennonite tourist destinations—offers an instructive case study. The site began its life in the early eighteenth century as a commune built by radical, millenarian Swiss-German Protestants who emigrated from Europe seeking freedom from religious persecution. The commune lasted until the early nineteenth century and then disbanded. In 1941, after a sustained period of deterioration, the site came under the jurisdiction of the Pennsylvania Historical and Museum Commission (PHMC). Initially, interpreters derived the Cloister's historical legitimacy from the folk art produced by its original inhabitants as well as its unique medieval Germanic architecture. Interpretive efforts followed suit. However, since 2000, a coordinated effort by site staff, religious studies scholars, archeologists, and the PHMC has resulted in an innovative reinterpretation of the site that centralizes its religious significance. Archeological and archival research yielded new information about the everyday lives and distinctive religious beliefs and practices of the site's original inhabitants, providing new fodder for educational tours and exhibits. Meanwhile, a staff-led endeavor reframed the Cloister's mission to focus on its significance as "a site . . . of religious toleration and intellectual freedom in the New World." Religion now intersects with older interpretive foci, such as folklore and architecture, within the site narrative. Site staff report that the change, although not without challenges, resonates with the public at large, the region, and local vested interests.[22] As the Cloister demonstrates, state-funded commemorative sites can successfully introduce a sacred or "private" past into broader historical narratives.

NEW APPROACHES TO OLD CONVERSATIONS

The entwined histories of commemoration and religion suggest that heritage professionals concerned with these themes will encounter deep-seated expectations in their audiences, both secular and faithful. And given the ubiquity of religion in American life—in politics, foreign policy, economics, athletics, popular culture, and elsewhere—institutions of public memory cannot afford to ignore it. As Peter Manseau, curator of religion at the Smithsonian Institution, puts it, "you can't tell the story of America . . . without the role of religion in it."[23] Doing so has real costs. For instance, rising turnout at the forthrightly ideological Creation Museum in Petersburg, Kentucky—occurring amid declining attendance rates at other museums and historical sites—suggests that heritage professionals need to take religion more seriously.[24]

Yet because of the varied modes by which religion filters into American life, it may not be immediately clear how would-be commemorators can provide new points of access into old and complex conversations. Our brief overview, however, suggests at least a few ways to get started, and perhaps some strategies for imagining a new path for this distinctive commemorative genre.

First, be collaborative. The reinterpretation of the Ephrata Cloister since 2000 suggests the power of partnerships—between museum professionals, scholars, administrators, and others—in improving commemorative projects. But even more modest projects can benefit from reaching out and working together. For instance, a committee planning a church or synagogue anniversary celebration might reach out to other area congregations for advice on what worked—and what did not—in their projects. The Congregational Library and Archives even encourages churches to focus their anniversary celebrations externally, beyond the walls of the church building, by partnering with community organizations and public service agencies. They suggest that the congregation tie "a person or event in your church history to a community project like fixing up the local cemetery or improving the neighborhood playground."[25] In these ways and others, collaboration can strengthen commemorative efforts.

Second, know your audience(s). For those developing private-made-public projects, this means knowing who you are trying to reach and planning accordingly. You should craft narratives that will resonate with your audience or audiences, and you should provide opportunities for audience engagement—either in the planning stages, or in the assessment stages, or both. Yet even as you work with a target audience or audiences in mind, do not be afraid to challenge your visitors. Differing viewpoints and new ideas can inspire and provoke. A commemorative project that leaves participants in the same state in which they entered subverts the power of the past.

For the public historians who create public-made-private projects, "knowing your audience(s)" might seem like trite advice. After all, the modus operandi for innovative practitioners these days is "letting go," giving up expert privilege in order to invite broad participation from diverse audiences—including, perhaps, religious audiences.[26] Yet as previously noted, public historians have a variety of reasons for not incorporating religion into exhibits, memorials, and other projects.

Even so, you would be better equipped to connect with wider audiences if you paid greater attention to the ways in which the epiphenomenal and the ineffable shape many Americans' engagement with the past. After all, public memory is often formed in the crucible of religious emotion—a fact made evident by the myriad references to "sacredness" that dominate the discourses of many battlefields, birthplaces, and other sites of public memory. Almost two decades ago, Rosenzweig's and Thelen's findings challenged us to reach bigger audiences by taking seriously the so-called intimate past.[27] Now, we will be better equipped to reach still larger audiences by taking seriously America's religious past—and its religious present.

NOTES

1. Christopher Cantwell, "Exhibiting Faith: Religion & Public History, Part 1," *Religion in American History* blog, March 8, 2013, http://usreligion.blogspot.com/2013/03/exhibiting-faith-religion-public.html.

2. John Seeyle, *Memory's Nation: The Place of Plymouth Rock* (Chapel Hill: The University of North Carolina Press, 1998), 33–34, and Robert D. Arner, "Plymouth Rock Revisited: The Landing of the Pilgrim Fathers," *Journal of American Culture* 6, no. 4 (Winter 1983), 26.

3. For more on history as a tool for expressing national pride during the first half of the nineteenth century, see Michael Kammen, *Mystic Chords of Memory: The Transformation of Tradition in American Culture* (New York: Vintage Books, 1991), 52–56, 62–90. On the origin and development of local history writing, see David J. Russo, *Keepers of Our Past: Local Historical Writing in the United States, 1820s–1930s* (New York: Greenwood Press, 1988); and Carol Kammen, *On Doing Local History*, 2nd ed. (Lanham, MD: AltaMira Press, 2003), 11–41.

4. John Franklin Stonecipher, *History of the Presbyterian Church of Dover, Delaware—A Sermon Preached on the Re-opening of the Church, October 23, 1887* MS 142, (Philadelphia, PA: Presbyterian Historical Society, 1887).

5. Margaret Bendroth, *The Last Puritans: Mainline Protestants and the Power of the Past* (Chapel Hill: The University of North Carolina Press, 2015), 18–25.

6. For instance, the Presbyterian Historical Society formed in 1852; the Congregational Library in 1853. See Virginia F. Raney, *Stewards of Our Heritage: A History of the Presbyterian Historical Society* (Louisville, KY: Geneva Press, 2002), and "About the Collection," Congregational Library, accessed May 15, 2016, www.congregationallibrary.org/about/collection. On the founding of historical societies in America, see Russo, *Keepers of Our Past,* 10–12, 80–82, and 192–193.

7. For a general overview of the transformation of America's religious landscape during the nineteenth century, see John Corrigan and Winthrop S. Hudson, *Religion in America*, 8th ed. (Boston, MA: Prentice Hall, 2010), 108–166, and Edwin S. Gaustad, *Historical Atlas of Religion in America*, 2nd ed. (New York: Harper & Row, 1976), 4.

8. Beth Wenger, *History Lessons: The Creation of American Jewish Heritage* (Princeton, NJ: Princeton University Press, 2010), 2.

9. Keith A. Erekson, "Memories, Monuments, and Mormonism: The Birthplace of Joseph Smith in Vermont," in Seth C. Bruggemann, ed. *Born in the U.S.A.: Birth, Commemoration, and Public Memory* (Amherst: University of Massachusetts Press, 2012), 131–151; Kathleen Flake, "Re-Placing Memory: Latter-Day Saint Use of Historical Monuments and Narrative in the Early Twentieth Century," *Religion and American Culture* 13, no. 1 (Winter 2003), 69–109; and Lindsay Adamson Livingston, "'This Is the Place': Performance and the Production of Space in Mormon Cultural Memory," in Scott Magelssen and Rhonda Justice-Malloy, eds. *Enacting History* (Tuscaloosa.: The University of Alabama Press, 2011), 22–40.

10. Erekson, *Born in the U.S.A.,* 133.

11. Quoted in Edward T. Linenthal, *Sacred Ground: Americans and Their Battlefields*, 2nd ed. (Urbana: University of Illinois Press, 1993).

12. For instance, Diane Barthel has argued that in nineteenth-century America "[historical] preservation initially served as one means of social integration: not just of classes but, equally important, of the increasingly diverse racial and ethnic populations. The homes of local heroes, revolutionary leaders, and of presidents were meant to teach civic obedience both to new generations and to new immigrants." See Barthel, *Historic Preservation: Collective Memory and Historical Identity* (New Brunswick, NJ: Rutgers University Press, 1996), 33.

13. In invoking this turn of phrase, I acknowledge my debt to Tammy Gordon's excellent *Private History in Public: Exhibition and the Settings of Everyday Life* (Lanham, MD: AltaMira, 2010).

14. Gordon offers a description and analysis of this genre of religious commemoration in Ibid., 46–47.

15. For example, the Flower Pentecostal Heritage Center in Springfield, Missouri, describes its mission as presenting "the Assemblies of God [Church] to our constituency in such a way as to create a joy of belonging and confidence in the mission, vision, and future of the Assemblies of God." See "Museum," Flower Pentecostal Heritage Center. https://ifphc.org/index.cfm?fuseaction=museum.main, accessed on May 23, 2016. By contrast, some similar institutions attempt to *collapse* the insider/outsider binary. The permanent exhibition on display at the Hebrew Union Congregation in Greenville, Mississippi, for example, interweaves national and international events, such as World War II and the Holocaust, with "community and personal history" to present the story of the region's Jewish population as one part of a broader set of narratives. In so doing, they link the specific stories of religious insiders with themes that may resonate with non-Jews viewing the exhibits. See the description of the exhibition in Gordon, *Private History in Public,* 46–47. Quotation from 46.

16. For example, the Mormon Church's Hill Cumorah Pageant, held annually in Palmyra, New York, near the site of church founder Joseph Smith's family farm, presents the community's history in such a way as to invite non-Mormons to "come feel the Savior's love," according to the pageant website. See "Hill Cumorah Pageant," HillCumorah.org, accessed May 15, 2016, http://www.hillcumorah.org/pageant_welcome.php. For a folklorist's analysis of the evangelistic function of the pageant, see Ellen E. McHale, "'Witnessing for Christ': The Hill Cumorah Pageant of Palmyra, New York," *Western Folklore* 44, no. 1 (January 1985), 34–40.

17. Ibid., 38.

18. Ibid., 50.

19. Ibid.

20. Cantwell, "Exhibiting Faith." On the History Wars, see Edward T. Linenthal and Tom Engelhardt, eds. *History Wars: The* Enola Gay *and Other Battles for the American Past* (New York: Henry Holt & Co., 1996).

21. National Park Service, U.S. Department of the Interior, "Part 60.4: Criteria for Evaluation," *Codes of Federal Regulations*, Title 36: Parks, Forests, and Public Property (2012), 335–336, https://www.gpo.gov/fdsys/pkg/CFR-2012-title36-vol1/pdf/CFR-2012-title36-vol1-part60.pdf

22. Darin D. Lenz, "History, Theology, and Interpretation: The Ephrata Cloister: A Case Study in Public History," *Concept* 26 (2003), https://concept.journals.

villanova.edu/article/view/317/280. For more on the history of the Cloister, see Jeff Bach, *Voices of the Turtledoves: The Sacred World of Ephrata* (University Park: The Pennsylvania State University Press, 2003). For more on the site itself, see http://www.ephratacloister.org/.

23. Julie Zauzmer, "The Smithsonain Now Has Its First Religion Curator since the 1890s," *The Washington Post*, October 28, 2016, https://www.washingtonpost.com/news/acts-of-faith/wp/2016/10/28/the-smithsonian-now-has-its-first-religion-curator-since-the-1890s/, accessed December 31, 2016.

24. Reports published by the American Alliance of Museums (2013) and the National Awareness, Attitudes, and Usage Study (2014) indicate that America's non-profit cultural institutions—including art and history museums, among others—have experienced declining attendance and concomitant declines in revenue. Meanwhile, the Creation Museum—a psuedoscientific, Young Earth creationist institution operated by the Christian apologetics organization Answers in Genesis—in 2015 reported annual attendance in excess of 287,000 visitors, marking "the eighth consecutive year that annual attendance exceeded the original . . . goal of 250,000 per year." On decline among nonprofit cultural institutions, see "America's Museums Reflect Slow Economic Recovery in 2012," American Alliance of Museums, https://www.aam-us.org/docs/research/acme-2013-final.pdf?sfvrsn=2, accessed December 31, 2016; and Colleen Dilenschneider, "Signs of Trouble for the Museum Industry," ColleenDilen.com, http://colleendilen.com/2014/12/03/signs-of-trouble-for-the-museum-industry-data/, accessed December 31, 2016; on the Creation Museum attendance, see "2015 Annual Report," AnswersInGenesis.org, https://assets.answersingenesis.org/doc/articles/about/annual-report-2015.pdf, accessed December 31, 2016.

25. "New Life from Old Stories: Anniversary Celebrations That Make a Difference," Congregational Library and Archives, accessed May 27, 2016, http://www.congregationallibrary.org/churches/anniversaries

26. On shared authority in public history, see Michael Fritsch, *A Shared Authority: Essays on the Craft and Meaning of Oral and Public History* (Albany: State University of New York Press, 1990), and Bill Adair, Benjamin Filene, and Laura Koloski, eds. *Letting Go? Sharing Authority in a User-Generated World* (Philadelphia, PA: The Pew Center for Arts and Heritage, 2011).

27. Roy Rozensweig and David Thelen, *The Presence of the Past: Popular Uses of History in American Life* (New York: Columbia University Press, 1998). On the reception of Rosenzweig and Thelen's work, see the essays in *The Public Historian* 22, no. 1 (Winter 2000) and James B. Gardner, "Contested Terrain: History, Museums, and the Public," *The Public Historian* 26, no. 4 (Fall 2004), 11–21.

Figure 11.1.   Pastor Harry Moore, Sr., of Mount Olive Baptist Church, presides over the eulogy of a soon-to-be-demolished rowhome in Mantua, West Philadelphia, May 31, 2014. Photo by Jeffrey Stockbridge.

Chapter 11

Commemoration as Activism

Patrick Grossi

For years now history workers across the spectrum of professional prac-tice have worried over the future of the past, and with good reason. His-tory professors struggle amid declining enrollments and an abysmal job market for new PhDs. The National Park Service's history corps labors beneath crushing maintenance backlogs and crippling budgetary restric-tions. Site managers and museum curators everywhere ponder off-mission programming to make ends meet and to keep visitors coming through the door. Representatives of all of these have even joined in a so-called History Relevance Campaign to convince Americans that history is, well, still relevant. And yet, at the same time, a fresh new current of historical awareness has percolated especially among young people at the periphery of these older vestiges of our nation's heritage infrastructure. In urban places particularly, where the politics of disinvestment have triggered powerful backlash, young activists can be found responding to inequity with an arsenal of historical tools. What sets them apart, as Patrick Grossi shows us by profiling standout examples of commemorative activism in Philadelphia, Pennsylvania, is a refusal to be content with relevance. At issue, rather, is the possibility of doing history born of radical empathy. "Commemorative activism," in Grossi's view, is not only possible, but "may offer the only responsible path forward."

—ed.

As this volume demonstrates, commemoration takes many forms. Yet, as Tammy Gordon suggests in chapter 2, the act of commemoration typi-cally operates in one of two ways (sometimes both): acts of *celebration* and acts of *mourning*. Whichever form they take, they are explicitly a remembrance, a marking, and forceful act of remembering. Both forms, celebration and mourning, invite an activist streak. But are they, in fact, works of activism? "Activism" implies a transparent political compass, a willful desire to enact social and political change. Demonstrations, petitions, marches, and advocacy campaigns are all conspicuous works of activism. Can history, a field that prides itself in disinterested observation, figure into the work of commemorative activism? Recent examples suggest a way forward.

What these case studies reveal is that history and commemoration can indeed be leveraged toward social justice. In fact, they suggest that amidst perilous times and broad skepticism concerning the relevance of historic sites, commemorative activism may offer the only responsible path forward for practitioners and the public alike. In the best tradition of public history, theirs is an *applied* history, a history that demonstrates its relevance to its intended audience, and even challenges the assumptions of audiences further afield. It is unapologetically political and reflective of the expanding narrative of the American experience and the people who populate it. These works are also, at their core, works of empathy. Whether a public spectacle, a pop-up art show, or an in-depth exhibit, the critical and emotional foundation of this work (and it is both critical *and* emotional) is a recognition of people's shared and unique experiences. Often, it is also a recognition of their pain. In sum, it is a recognition of their humanity.

On the face of it, that should not be too hard a pill to swallow for most historians. This is simply another means of measuring and documenting human agency, one of the core inquiries of professional historians. What is different is that the typical priorities are inverted. Careful research and analysis of group behavior and circumstance can often result in increased sympathy for individuals or groups. A thorough understanding of the collective struggles of African Americans over the long course of the American experiment, in turn, influences one's moral political compass in the present. The work discussed here operates in reverse. It emerged first from a desire and capacity for greater empathy, and even more ambitiously, social change. The greater understanding and documentation that resulted is in some respects, "gravy," but it was likewise made possible by the empirical work of historical inquiry. If this sounds a bit touchy feely, well, it should. Its institutional forebears are people such as Freeman Tilden, the celebrated NPS interpreter who emphasized love, compassion, and provocation; "Mr." Fred Rogers, America's security blanket and window into emotional intelligence; and Dolores Hayden, whose inversion of preservation philosophy at the turn of the twentieth century is still just maturing. Upon closer inspection, though, the reader may start to recognize that these impulses aren't all that radical. In fact, they are quite common.

THE BIG GRAPH, EASTERN STATE PENITENTIARY

Eastern State Penitentiary's *Prisons Today: Questions in the Age of Mass Incarceration* is a radical work of museum advocacy. Opened in the spring of 2016, the exhibit ambitiously seeks to answer head on the question that always loomed just under the surface of its long-standing interpretive model: How does an 1829 prison that in its own day revolutionized the rehabilitative role of prisons reconcile with a contemporary culture of mass incarceration and penalizing of nonviolent crimes that most heavily impacts citizens of non-white and low-income backgrounds? This image shows "The Big Graph," a precursor to the official 2016 exhibit, which commemorates the dramatic rise in U.S. incarceration rates since 1970. By combining quantitative data with graphically ambitious works of sculpture and interpretive panels, "Prisons Today" models the play, provocation, and radical pedagogy embedded in today's commemorative activism.

Figure 11.2. The Big Graph, Eastern State Penitentiary (see sidebar for full caption). Photo by Rob Hashem. Courtesy of Eastern State Penitentiary Historic Site.

As I write this, a ceremony is being planned in Jersey City, New Jersey, to mark the one hundredth anniversary of the infamous "Black Tom" explosion, a 1916 act of sabotage by German conspirators resulting in seven casualties. Here in Philadelphia, work is underway to create a memorial park on the site of a 2013 building collapse that killed six people. Activist commemoration often invokes somber pasts. State markers across the City of Philadelphia recognize the harsh realities of the city's heritage. A marker at 6th and Race Sts. recognizes the former site of Pennsylvania Hall, the then newly constructed meeting

PHILADELPHIA PUBLIC HISTORY TRUCK

Erin Bernard's Philadelphia Public History Truck merges the work of oral history, public outreach, and pop-up exhibitory to create new narratives of the Philadelphia experience. A place-based, neighborhood-centric practice, the Truck has intentionally focused on areas that have experienced and continue to experience both disinvestment and dramatic change. Though its methods are not new, its merger of local history, participant-observation, and articulation of the past through visual art have rightly captured the attention of historians and artists both locally and nationally. Bernard's work also intentionally blurs the line between recorder of the past and contemporary advocate.

Figure 11.3.   The Philadelphia Public History Truck (see sidebar for full caption). Laura S. Kicey.

place of the Pennsylvania Anti-Slavery Society that in 1838 was burned to the ground by nativist and pro-slavery rioters. In many ways, it is the willingness to acknowledge such sad moments that is, itself, a work of activism.

Commemorative activism is also often simply a recognition of past political action. As if anticipating Kenneth Turino's call to action in chapter 9, two new historical markers were erected in the City of Philadelphia in July 2016 to recognize the efforts of early LGBT activists in the 1970s, markers reflective of a national push to better document and recognize LGBT history. Martin Luther King's 1965 "Freedom Now" rally is commemorated at the intersection of 40th St. and Lancaster Avenue in West Philadelphia, via a state marker, statuary, and city-sanctioned mural (a commemoration trifecta). An activist impulse has long been innate in the work of history and public commemoration.

Historic preservation, my current field of employment, increasingly serves as a natural arena for commemorative activism. Preservation is most typically associated with efforts to recognize and restore significant works of architecture. But implicit in the work of historic preservation, particularly in large cities such as my hometown Philadelphia, is the complicated landscape of resident desires, municipal zoning, erratic real estate markets, and here in America, allegedly inalienable property rights. These battles are most pronounced amidst local efforts to have buildings legally deemed historic and listed on the Philadelphia Register of Historic Places (which prohibits demolition and regulates future alterations). A claim to a historic building, made by a concerned citizen or recognized nonprofit parties who often do not own the building or have any direct financial stake in the property, is a radical claim of public ownership and commonweal. It suggests that history, narrative and its physical manifestations, even the subjective beauty of the built environment, trump the right to maximizing private profit and responsibly regulate private freedoms. In legal terms, it can occasionally be characterized as a "taking," though the jurisprudence on takings law is largely in favor of past historic preservation efforts.

There is, however, one consistent thread through each of these projects, not yet discussed: a willingness and interest in using the language and methods of visual arts to deliver the message and meaning of history and commemoration. Broadly defined as "social practice" (among other terms of art), the concept is by no means new to the arts. What is new, however, is the institutionalization of this practice, so much so that some social practice artists worry increased institutionalization and defining of best practices will compromise the original intentions of the approach itself. In short, the art world is having its "public history" moment, a moment when practitioners are questioning the utility of their institutions, and making conscious efforts to engage directly with the social, political, and economic realities of their towns and cities.

FUNERAL FOR A HOME

Presented as "a demolition in the service of preservation," Temple Contemporary's Funeral for a Home is a radical work of preservation activism. Over the course of 2013–2014, the author, local artists Billy and Steven Dufala, and curators at Temple University sought to commemorate a vacant rowhome in its, presumably, last year of existence. Oral history and public outreach work conducted over the better part of a year culminated in a public memorial service for the 142-year-old house in Mantua, West Philadelphia, a service informed by both local traditions and the personal legacies of the home and those who inhabited it. At the service's conclusion, the rowhome's cornice was ceremoniously removed and the structure demolished later that day. Newly constructed affordable housing units and a dedicated facility for the Mantua Civic Association are currently being planned for the former site of the home.

Figure 11.4.   Funeral for a Home (see sidebar for full caption). Photo by Jeffrey Stockbridge.

In recent years, I have had the good fortune to engage in this work directly, both as an observer and a practitioner. Increasingly, the work seems to lend itself to urban contexts, particularly in postindustrial cities such as Philadelphia, Baltimore, and Chicago. That's not to suggest it is purely an urban phenomenon. It is simply a new and maturing method of engaging the past, accomplished by thinking seriously about our efforts to engage audiences and the willingness to embrace interdisciplinarity. We would be well to do so not to simply "disrupt" best practices, or challenge assumptions for challenge's sake. More to the point, these projects demonstrate a remarkable ability to cultivate and foster historical consciousness. If such is the mark of a truly successful historian, and I believe strongly that it is, commemorative activism offers the signpost toward that laudable goal.

Figure 12.1.   Young visitor enjoying the opening of special commemorative exhibit *Civil War Pathways in the Pacific Northwest* at the Washington State History Museum on February 17, 2014. Musician and frontier-era reenactor Patrick Haas playing a replica of a traditional, homemade, 1835 five-string banjo, made of rawhide skin stretched over a gourd. Courtesy of the Washington State Historical Society.

Chapter 12

Alive in Our Imagination

The Sesquicentennial of the American Civil War

Rick Beard and Bob Beatty

Despite efforts—by activists and others—to shift our commemorative habits, public memory is stubbornly resistant to change. Consider, for instance, the great commemorative dilemma of our time: how to remember the American Civil War. That the war has echoed throughout several preceding chapters speaks to its ubiquity in American life and memory. And yet Americans seem impossibly divided over its legacy. Should we, as some suggest, focus our commemorative gaze squarely on the four years during which Americans warred against one another, or ought we think more broadly about the causes and aftermaths of this nation's pivotal nightmare? Tempting though it may be to disregard what seems like an intractable debate, we learn from Cathy Stanton, George McDaniel, and many others beyond this volume, that the stakes in this memory battle are too grave to ignore. Rick Beard and Bob Beatty seek here to advance the conversation by considering how Civil War commemoration has—and has not—evolved since the war's centennial celebration over a half century ago. While their survey of efforts surrounding the more recent Civil War sesquicentennial may give some cause for optimism, it makes clear too that core challenges remain.

—ed.

The novelist William Faulkner famously observed, "The past is not dead. In fact, it's not even past." If he was not thinking of the Civil War when he penned these sentences, he might as well have been. From the moment that Robert E. Lee rode away from the McLean home in Appomattox Court House on April 9, 1865, Americans began arguing over the causes and consequences of the Civil War, or, if you prefer, the War of the Rebellion, the War Between the States, or the War of Northern Aggression. What a person chooses to name this bloodletting that cost at least 750,000 American lives

says everything about an individual's sectional affiliation. Robert Penn Warren, in his 1961 essay *The Legacy of the Civil War*, characterized the war as
"our felt history—history lived in the national imagination."[1]

Despite its central place in our nation's historical imagination, common
ground for interpreting and remembering the war has continually eluded
Americans. Noted historian Gary Gallagher observed that when understanding the conflict, "the wider issue is how the Civil War should be presented to
the American people, and why academic and popular conceptions about the
conflict are often so different."[2] For many public historians, the occasion of
the war's 150th anniversary—the sesquicentennial years between 2011 and
2015—presented an opportunity to narrow this conceptual gap among Americans by offering fresh perspectives on the many controversies that surround
the conflict and how we remember it.

Our purpose in this chapter is to assess how well they did. We begin by
considering the sesquicentennial's commemorative context. Planners struggled with the difficult task of harnessing profound public interest in an event
that had no useful precedent in previous commemorations. What is more,
unanticipated shortages of funds and the absence of national leadership called
for creative thinking on the part of state and local organizations interested in
commemorating the war's 150th anniversary. With all of this in mind, we
survey nine of the thirty states that hosted events commemorating the 150th
anniversary of the Civil War.[3] Alongside a consideration, too, of the(NPS
efforts, we propose some preliminary conclusions about the successes and
shortcomings of the Sesquicentennial.

THE CIVIL WAR CENTENNIAL
AS PROBLEMATIC PRECEDENT

In 1957, President Dwight D. Eisenhower established the U.S. Civil War
Centennial Commission. From the outset, an unspoken expectation that
the Commission support the nation's ideological battles with its Cold War
adversaries shaped its efforts. Historian Robert Cook has documented how
the Centennial chose to overlook problematic aspects of the American past
and failed to draw historical parallels that today seem self-evident. Most
egregiously, Centennial events failed to explore the linkages between slavery
and emancipation during the 1860s and the divisive civil rights issues that
were roiling contemporary American society and providing ammunition for
the nation's foreign adversaries.[4] Nor did the Eisenhower administration or
Congress seem eager to articulate a unifying national theme for the Sesquicentennial, thereby leaving individual states to define the commemoration
for themselves.

After Allan Nevins, a Pulitzer Prize-winning historian, replaced U.S. Grant III, the Union general's grandson, as chairman of the commission in late 1961, an initial enthusiasm for large-scale battle reenactments quickly gave way to a programmatic focus on education.[5] Cook argues that the Commission's educational impulses sometimes ran afoul of the same sensitivities that had inflamed sectional passions one hundred years earlier. This was especially true in the South, where state commissions often exploited the Centennial to justify a distinctive southern "way of life," characterized by rigid segregation, as a response to black agitation for equal rights. The Centennial's lack of success in educating the public about the causes and consequences of the Civil War, Cook argues, represented a significant missed opportunity.[6]

While the Centennial's commemorative and educational offerings were generally disappointing, and though representatives from history museums were notably absent in their planning, the NPS was able to leverage the occasion to secure Congressional appropriations with which to reimagine many Civil War battlefields. New visitor centers, interpretive films and exhibitions, and onsite signage all helped visitors better understand what had transpired one hundred years earlier. But the interpretive focus was almost entirely on the war's military aspects. Absent were considerations of the home front, the role that women played, and the destruction of slavery.[7]

By the end of the twentieth century, however, public interest in and knowledge about the Civil War had grown considerably. Historian James M. McPherson's Civil War chronicle, *Battle Cry of Freedom* (1988), won a Pulitzer Prize and sold more than 600,000 copies. Ken Burns's *The Civil War* (1990) television series attracted over fourteen million viewers. By the end of the decade, over forty million people had seen at least one of its nine episodes.[8] A dramatic transformation in Civil War historiography helped feed the public's growing appetite. Historians wrestled with new questions about causation, slavery and race, personal motivation, leadership, memory, and legacy rarely explored by an earlier generation of historians.[9] University and commercial presses churned out books on the Civil War at a record pace. No subject seemed too obscure to attract the interest of experts, buffs, and newcomers alike.

PLANNING THE CIVIL WAR SESQUICENTENNIAL

Despite an upsurge in popular interest, Congress failed to create a federal commission to coordinate the war's 150th anniversary. Deliberations in the U.S. Senate had begun in 1996, when it designated the Civil War Center at Louisiana State University as the flagship institution for Sesquicentennial planning.[10] Bills proposed in successive congresses, however, never made it out of the National Parks Subcommittee. The AASLH convened an eleventh-hour meeting in April 2009 that led to the formation of an ad hoc Civil War Sesquicentennial Coalition. Fourteen national organizations agreed to press the White House to create a presidential commission to coordinate the anniversary.[11] The coalition assembled a statement of purpose, a management plan, and an advisory council of one hundred of the nation's leading Civil War scholars.[12] But with no response from the White House, the coalition turned to Democratic Senators Mary Landrieu (Los Angeles) and James Webb (Virginia), sponsors of legislation to create a congressional commission. This last-ditch effort came to naught, too, when Congress failed to act.

Responsibility for commemorating a significant Civil War anniversary would thus fall to state and local institutions. The AASLH had, in fact, begun engaging its membership about how best to commemorate the Sesquicentennial several years earlier. A roundtable at its 2006 annual meeting focused on seeking common ground among various Civil War stakeholders: public historians, academic scholars, collectors, reenactors and other buffs, and heritage groups such as the Sons of the Confederate Veterans. Three sessions at the 2007 annual meeting tackled the challenge head on. In a plenary address, historian David Blight discussed the difference between "memory" of the past and "history." In a follow-up discussion, Blight and Dwight Pitcaithley, former chief historian for the NPS, warned planners against focusing on battlefield valor and noble reunions between North and South lest they risk splintering the Sesquicentennial among different interest groups. At a third session, AASLH members produced four recommendations for member organizations planning Sesquicentennial activities: emphasize the 150 years of history since 1861, not the 150th anniversary of the war; share primary sources with the public that illustrate the war's causes and effects; be centers for open discourse about the war and its legacy; and, respect, hear, and engage all groups.[13]

And yet, basic questions still loomed. Who, for instance, would provide leadership in the absence of a national commission? Ultimately, leadership came from a variety of sources. During 2009–2012, for instance, the AASLH hosted quarterly conference calls with as many as twenty-five representatives from state historical agencies, federal agencies such as the National Endowment for the Humanities (NEH) and the NPS, and private not-for-profits such as the Civil War Trust.[14] Several states created official commissions that played an active role in shaping programs. Others created advisory committees, which generally had little authority to determine the specifics of any particular activity. Still others assigned responsibility to a state agency, such as the archives, or to the state historical society, which in several cases were private not-for-profit organizations. Among the nine states surveyed for this chapter, six had official commissions or advisory groups.[15] In the other three, the state's historical society or archive took the lead in shaping commemorative events.

Leadership notwithstanding, questions also remained about how to pay for commemorative programing amid a dire economic landscape. The 2008 financial crisis virtually guaranteed little to no new funding from federal or state sources. Only Virginia and Pennsylvania received significant state funding— $7.4 and $6.4 million, respectively—for commemorative events. No other state provided more than $500,000, usually from tourism or economic development budgets. In three of the states surveyed—Pennsylvania, Virginia, and Georgia—the NEH and the Institute for Museum and Library Services invested heavily in exhibitions and education programs. Virginia also raised $1.69 million from private sources, and Connecticut received $200,000 from Traveler's Insurance for several of its programs. But significant support from foundations and corporations was not forthcoming.[16] The 150th anniversary of the Civil War failed to attract the sort of robust financial support from private sources that had fueled, for instance, the America Bicentennial (1976) and the Statue of Liberty Centenary (1986).

THE SESQUICENTENNIAL IN THEORY AND PRACTICE

Funding limitations and the absence of coordination at the national level, however, failed to dissuade America's history organizations from commemorating the 150th anniversary of the Civil War.[17] On the contrary, many state history organizations and NPS planners, too, embraced the AASLH's challenge to emphasize change over time in the 150 years since the war's beginning rather than to focus, as the Centennial had, on anniversaries of battles and events. Three considerations shaped this commitment: the recognition that the Centennial had played out in a historical vacuum unrelated to 1960s America; an awareness that current scholarship made it impossible not to reckon with the ongoing consequences of the Civil War; and a desire to engage African Americans in a consideration of the historical interplay between the Civil War and the civil rights movement one hundred years later. A review of Sesquicentennial highlights in nine states, however, suggests that this commitment was honored more in word than in deed.

Some of the most well-funded commemorative programming occurred in Virginia and Pennsylvania. The Virginia Sesquicentennial of the American Civil War Commission—the nation's most ambitious state program—sponsored exhibitions, conferences, and online resources that featured the latest scholarship on military strategy and leadership, race and slavery, the home front, and causes and consequences. Especially noteworthy were seven "Signature Conferences" that averaged nearly 1,000 participants.[18] Pennsylvania's state-supported *Civil War 150*, a short-lived mobile exhibition, similarly explored the war's impact on civilians and soldiers alike. The Senator John Heinz History Center, the state's largest history museum, organized several exhibitions, some traveling, and also oversaw a robust publishing initiative.[19]

Ohio's sesquicentennial programming aimed to recall "the war's importance in our history and reflect upon its enduring legacy in our lives."[20] An ambitious roster of exhibitions and educational programs focused primarily on the Civil War years, but participants did have opportunities to consider the war's long-term impact on the state.[21] Connecticut's sesquicentennial efforts also displayed a consistent focus on the war. Highlights included Civil War encampments, which enlisted the state's large reenactor community in a partnership with academic historians to present programs with a broad appeal. Slavery and race also received special programming attention.[22]

Deep South states such as South Carolina, Georgia, and Alabama faced unique challenges when commemorating the war's anniversary. South Carolina's history museum community was called on early in the Sesquicentennial to push back against polarizing events such as the 2010 Secession Ball in Charleston. While one white state legislator claimed that the celebration of the state's secession ordinance was "in our DNA," the vice president of the local National Association for the Advancement of Colored People (NAACP) chapter characterized the event as "disgusting." The Sesquicentennial, observed one reporter, would provide Americans with "ample opportunities to wrestle with delicate, almost-impossible-to-resolve questions of legacy and history, of what to commemorate and what to condemn."[23]

South Carolina's *Civil War 150* advisory board did indeed wrestle with one of the South's most pervasive shibboleths, the myth of the Lost Cause. *Confrontation to Conflict: South Carolina's Path to the Civil War*, for example, used primary documents to illustrate how the signers of South Carolina's 1860 "Declaration of Immediate Causes," which accompanied the secession proclamation, themselves identified slavery as the cause for disunion. And yet, though other programs linked the Civil War with the modern civil rights movement, these connections "felt very forced" in the opinion of Eric Emerson, the state advisory board's chair and director of the South Carolina Department of Archives and History.[24] Georgia's programming, though focused tightly on the four-year period of the war, featured a series of historical markers created by the Georgia Historical Society that challenged old interpretive narratives, and did so on a minimalist budget. Unlike in Virginia or South Carolina, however, Georgia did not mount a major exhibit on the war, due perhaps to *Turning Point: The American Civil War*, a long-term exhibition on view at the Atlanta History Center that is generally ranked among the nation's very best.[25]

Alabama, conversely, fully embraced the AASLH's challenge. "Becoming Alabama," a statewide partnership overseen by the Department of Archives and History, commemorated major anniversaries of the Creek War and the War of 1812, the Civil War, and the civil rights movement, each of which had formative impacts on the state's history. In part, a response to budgetary restraints, and a move to encourage efficiencies in marketing, the wider interpretive focus of "Becoming Alabama" also effectually marginalized the impact of groups with a neo-Confederate view on the interpretation of the Civil War.

Although neither Washington nor Idaho played any direct role in the Civil War, both states used the Sesquicentennial as an opportunity to examine aspects of their own histories. In Washington a major exhibition, *The Civil War Experience in Washington Territory*, and a speaker's bureau stimulated wide-ranging public discussions about race and slavery, territorial wartime politics, the wartime suspension of habeas corpus and freedom of the press, international affairs in the Pacific, and the unpopularity of the Reconstruction amendments. As Janet Gallimore describes in chapter 6, Idaho's programming focused on its path to statehood in 1863 rather than on the particularities of the Civil War.[26]

As the conservator of more than seventy-five sites related to the Civil War, the NPS was especially well positioned to play a large role during the Sesquicentennial. A 2008 report recommended an interpretive approach that would challenge visitors "to not just understand the nature and horrid expanse of the bloodshed, but the reasons for it, and the consequences of its aftermath." Recognizing that "NPS sites relating to the Civil War are not exclusively battle sites," the plan expanded the "the accepted definition of what constitutes a Civil War site and proposed a more nuanced approach to interpretation . . . that goes beyond stereotypes toward a clearer (though more complex) understanding of the war."[27] Unfortunately, the NPS intention to broaden the narrative at its Civil War sites in time for the Sesquicentennial came up short when Congress failed to pass supplemental appropriations for the 150th anniversary. A change in top leadership also redirected its focus toward big events such as the commemoration of battle anniversaries rather than investment in new interpretive media.[28] NPS staff found themselves fighting an internal battle to revise an original vision statement for the Sesquicentennial that made no mention of slavery. The revised version called for a commemoration of events stretching from the Civil War to the civil rights movement.[29]

Just as planners struggled to expand the war's commemorative chronology, so did they have mixed success in promoting dialogue among various Civil War constituencies. Connecticut and Ohio built on existing relationships among reenactors and academic historians. The cochair of the Connecticut commission considered a series of annual encampments that attracted robust attendance and significant corporate support to be among the state's most successful Sesquicentennial activities.[30] Ohio's reenactor community played a key role in programming throughout the state. One particularly creative recreation of a sanitary fair illustrated the role that women played during the Civil War. But the marriage between reenactors and scholars was not without friction. Plans by one group of Ohio reenactors to display a Confederate flag led to an impasse when a commission member representing the Sons of Union Veterans (SUV) strenuously objected. When a historian attempted to mediate the dispute, the SUV representative insisted that "We don't need no egghead profs. . . . This is America." America or not, the flag's use was approved.[31]

Engaging more politically aggressive heritage organizations like the Sons of Confederate Veterans (SCV) proved impossible. A dialogue requires two sides willing to talk. Heritage groups like the SCV invariably chose instead to operate in a parallel universe, presenting programs of their own and generally refusing to engage with officially sanctioned commemorative events. Their interpretation of the Civil War was radically at odds with the prevailing scholarship. In an interview, the commander-in-chief of the SCV repeated the oft-made states' rights argument that people in the South "were only fighting to protect themselves from an invasion and for their independence." A SCV advertising campaign repeated the claim: "All we wanted was to be left alone to govern ourselves." The somewhat aghast president of the South Carolina NAACP responded that he could "only imagine what kind of celebration they would have if they had won." When Southerners refer to states' rights, he insisted, "They are really talking about their idea of one right—to buy and sell human beings."[32]

The "Secession Ball" in Charleston stoked fears that the ongoing controversy over the Confederate flag might mar the Sesquicentennial. But commemorative efforts in Alabama, Georgia, Virginia, and South Carolina generated little pushback from neo-Confederates. In the opinion of Eric Emerson, the Sesquicentennial marked "the last commemoration during which the Lost Cause will be an issue."[33] Controversies surrounding slavery and race, however, were far less muted during the Sesquicentennial. The Georgia Historical Society's fifteen new roadside historical markers, for instance, invited both praise and criticism. Four markers tell stories about the African American experience during the Civil War in Georgia.[34] The dedication of a marker near Dalton, concerning the only local battle in which blacks soldiers fought, drew over 300 people. Patricia Rivers, head of Dalton's black history society, explained that "Some people may not be aware that there were African-American soldiers who fought in the Civil War [or] didn't know that they fought right here in their hometown." Former Atlanta mayor Andrew Young noted that black soldiers had served honorably in every war the United States has fought, starting with the Revolutionary War.[35]

Some critics of the society and its markers warned that "talking about slavery only made it worse."[36] In the case of a marker on Martin Luther King, Jr. Drive commemorating the burning of Atlanta, the city's NAACP chapter responded that "We accept that [the war and slavery are] history but would like to see it done somewhere else other than the heart of the civil rights historic district."[37] Young succinctly captured the dilemma that the Atlanta NAACP head and many other blacks faced when confronting the commemoration of the Sesquicentennial. "We don't know what to commemorate because we've never faced up to the implications of what the thing was really about," he noted. "The easy answer for black folk is that it set us free, but it really didn't. We had another 100 years of segregation. We've never had our complete reconciliation of the forces that divide us."[38]

THE SESQUICENTENNIAL: SUCCESS OR DISAPPOINTMENT

What can we conclude about the commemoration of the 150th anniversary of the Civil War from this brief survey? Did the Sesquicentennial succeed or fall short of expectations? Were history museums successful in expanding the historical time frame to include more than the four years of the war? Did Sesquicentennial activities engage the wide range of audiences so eagerly sought after by professionals? None of the planners we spoke with felt that their efforts had been unsuccessful, although most recognized that they could have done a lot more with additional funding. It is worth noting, however, that the mere availability of money was no guarantee of success. Both Virginia and Pennsylvania received major state grants, but the former's menu of Sesquicentennial activities was the far richer and more varied of the two. And the Georgia Historical Society spent considerably less than $200,000 for a markers program that expanded the Civil War narrative in significant ways.

While institutions in all nine states expressed the desire to examine the connection between the Civil War and the civil rights movement, it is clear that the war received the lion's share of programmatic energy and most of the public's attention. The NPS fared better in this regard, but primarily because its sites already interpreted events spanning the 150-year time period. So, as an exercise in interpreting the Civil War, few could judge the Sesquicentennial as anything less than a success. But it largely failed to explore the war's broader consequences as they impacted the black struggle for equal rights over the succeeding century and a half. It also appears that history institutions rarely expanded their audiences beyond the "usual suspects" during the Sesquicentennial. The success both Ohio and Connecticut enjoyed working with reenactors and scholars represented the cross-fertilization of existing audiences, not the creation of new ones. In none of the nine states we surveyed were there meaningful interactions between history museums and heritage groups like the SCV. Ohio's experience with the SUV appears to have been anomalous.

Despite all of this, Sesquicentennial programs committed to identifying and digitizing historical documents seem to have made information about the Civil War more accessible than ever. Virginia's Civil War 150 Legacy Project, spearheaded by the Library of Virginia, searched through private collections to identify and locate letters, memoirs, diaries, hand-drawn maps, and selected memorabilia and other manuscripts related to the Civil War and emancipation. Since the project kicked off in 2009, it has digitized over 32,000 items in a collection honoring the noted Civil War historian James "Bud" Robertson, Jr.[39] In Georgia, the Atlanta History Center introduced a major collection of more than 600 rare Confederate firearms, edged weapons, flags, uniforms, and accouterments.[40] In Alabama, major projects included the preservation of Confederate battle flags, the digitization of service records, and the ongoing digitization of Civil War-era newspapers. Connecticut's commission, working with the state library, is documenting the Sesquicentennial itself by archiving commemorative materials that will interest planners and historians fifty years hence. This laudable effort should be duplicated elsewhere, particularly in this age of ephemeral digital communication, toward documenting how commemoration works at state and local levels.

So, did the sesquicentennial ameliorate differences in how we understand the war? Some, like Georgia Historical Society President Todd Groce, believe that the Sesquicentennial did help to bridge the gulf between public and academic history. Dwight Pitcaithley, on the other hand, once NPS chief historian and now a history professor at New Mexico State University, believes that the Sesquicentennial did not "move the dial much."[41] What most heritage professionals seem to agree on is that the Sesquicentennial's greatest failing was its inability to attract African American audiences. It was not for lack of trying. Many institutions created programs about slavery, emancipation, and the critical role of black troops calibrated to attract black visitors. Perhaps, as Andrew Young suggested, this was not enough. While white audiences generally feel comfortable celebrating a Civil War narrative that emphasizes black emancipation, for many in the African American community, the absence of a "complete reconciliation" remains a challenge, not just for those interpreting our nation's history but for the well-being of the American enterprise itself. In this sense, although the Civil War Sesquicentennial did provide glimpses into our "history lived in the national imagination," none of these were ultimately transformative.

CODA

In the weeks following the 2015 tragedy at Charleston's Mother Emanuel AME Church, chronicled in this volume by George W. McDaniel, the long-simmering dispute over the Confederate flag and other symbols of southern heritage seemed to have taken a turn. Retail giants such as Walmart, Sears, and Kmart announced plans to stop selling merchandise featuring the Confederate flag. Elected officials in Mississippi, Virginia, Tennessee, North Carolina, and Kentucky vowed to revisit the use of the flag and the placement of Confederate monuments. Despite protests by the SCV, which dismissed this soul-searching as "a feeding frenzy of cultural cleansing," the South Carolina legislature voted to remove the flag from outside the statehouse, and ordered it lowered for the final time. The pastor of a black Charleston congregation commented, "That flag is simply a start; that's all it is."[42]

It is tempting to suggest that the rapid transformation of the public discourse about Confederate symbols might be due, at least in part, to the Sesquicentennial. Did the exhibitions, lectures and symposia, school programs, reenactments, publications, and other activities commemorating the 150th anniversary of the Civil War prime us for a change of attitude? From his local perspective in South Carolina, Eric Emerson believes the Sesquicentennial had little to do with the flag's removal, suggesting instead that the presence of the Rev. Clementa C. Pinckney, a pastor and state senator, among the victims was decisive.[43] Robert Sutton, immediate past chief historian of the NPS, suggests from his national standpoint that the "rabids," as he labels the more extreme members of heritage groups like the SCV, "have lost their clout."[44]

Gauging the Sesquicentennial's impact in this regard is likely impossible. What is evident, however, is that less than nine months after the Charleston shootings, much of the enthusiasm for removing Confederate symbols seemed to have waned. "The pendulum has gone the other direction," noted a political consultant in Mississippi. "It's now about protecting [the symbols] and insulating them from future efforts, even after another Charleston-type shooting."[45] Indeed, surveys show that Confederate heritage remains a hot button issue for both white and black Americans, with over half of white Americans saying that the Confederate flag represents Southern pride rather than racism. In the South, three quarters of whites describe the flag as a symbol of pride, while the same percentage of blacks identify the flag with racism.[46]

If Faulkner was right, and the past is, in fact, "not even past," then what will it take to cause a sea change in attitudes toward the Civil War's causes and consequences? Our experience of the Sesquicentennial suggests no immediate answer. Those continuing to wrestle with the question must account for Americans' growing disinterest in historical nuance and their growing embrace of social media platforms that privilege information delivered immediately in bite-sized increments. Over 150 years later, we seem no closer to resolving Gary Gallagher's question of "how the Civil War should be presented to the American people."

NOTES

The authors thank the following for sharing information about their work during the Sesquicentennial. It goes without saying that the opinions expressed herein are those of the authors alone. Jackie Barton, chief program officer, Ohio History Connection; Dr. Eric Emerson, director, South Carolina Department of Archives and History; Barbara Franco, founding director Emerita, Gettysburg Seminary Ridge Museum; Janet Gallimore, executive director, Idaho State Historical Society; Dr. W. Todd Groce, president and chief executive officer (CEO), Georgia Historical Society; Cheryl Jackson, executive director, Virginia Sesquicentennial of the American Civil War Commission; Dr. Lorraine McConaghy, Public Historian Emeritus at the Museum of History and Industry in Seattle, and a lecturer in Museum Studies at the University of Washington; Steve Murray, director, Alabama Department of Archives and History; Dwight Pitcaithley and Robert Sutton, both former chief historians for the NPS; and Professor Matt Warschauer, chairperson, Connecticut Civil War Commemoration Committee, and professor of History, Central Connecticut State University.

1. The Faulkner quote is taken from *Requiem for a Nun*. Robert Penn Warren, *The Legacy of the Civil War* (Lincoln: University of Nebraska Press, 1998), 4.

2. Gary Gallagher, *Lee and His Generals in War and Memory* (Baton Rouge: Louisiana State University Press, 1998), viii.

3. The nine states surveyed were Alabama, Georgia, South Carolina, Virginia, Pennsylvania, Ohio, Connecticut, Washington, and Idaho.

4. Robert Cook, *Troubled Commemoration: The American Civil War Centennial, 1961–1965* (Baton Rouge, Louisiana State University Press, 2007), 81.

5. Grant was an anti-Semite and displayed remarkable tone deafness on racial issues, which led to embarrassing press coverage of some of the Commission's earliest meetings.

6. Cook, *Troubled Commemoration*, 13.

7. See Dwight Pitcaithley, "'A Cosmic Threat': The National Park Service Addresses the Causes of the American Civil War," in James Oliver Horton and Lois E. Horton, eds. *Slavery and Public History: The Tough Stuff of American Memory* (New York: W.W. Norton & Company, 2006), 169–187.

8. Drew Gilpin Faust, "'We Should Grow Too Fond of It': Why We Love the Civil War" (*Civil War History*, December 2004), 368–383. The rebroadcast of Burns' *The Civil War* several times during the intervening years and during the Sesquicentennial, as well as its availability on DVD, undoubtedly guaranteed that many millions more Americans had a chance to see it.

9. The older generation of historians included Allan Nevins, Shelby Foote, and Bruce Catton. The more recent generation included McPherson, Drew Gilpin Faust, David Blight, Eric Foner, Gary Gallagher, Catherine Clinton, Nina Silber, Edward Ayers, and many others.

10. The Civil War Center, organized in the mid-1990s, began life with ambitious plans to become a major resource. By 2011, it was no more than a small space in the university's special collections reading room. Successive versions of the legislation introduced additional institutions that were to take the lead in shaping the Sesquicentennial, most notably the National Civil War Museum in Harrisburg, Pennsylvania, and Pamplin Historical Park in Petersburg, Virginia. None of these institutions were equipped to provide national leadership for the 150th anniversary commemoration.

11. Members included the American Association for State and Local History, American Association of Museums (now the American Alliance of Museums), Association for the Study of African American Life and History, Civil War Trust, Federation of State Humanities Councils, Gettysburg Battlefield Memorial Foundation, the History Channel, National Coalition for History, National Council for the Social Studies, National History Day, National Trust for Historic Preservation, National Council on Public History, Society for Military History, and Southern Historical Association.

12. Cochaired by James McPherson, James Horton, and William Cooper

13. Blight's address can be accessed at http://resource.aaslh.org/view/david-blight-plenary-address-2007-aaslh-annual-meeting/. An account of the conference's discussions related to the Sesquicentennial can be found in Beth Hager, "The Civil War Sesquicentennial: Seeking Common Ground Conversations at the 2007 Annual Meeting," *History News* 63, no. 1 (Winter 2008), 16–19. Initial plans for this session had included the participation by a member of the SCV and a representative from the Southern Poverty Law Center. Unfortunately, neither individual chose to attend.

14. While periodic efforts within this group to promote regional or national collaborations failed to bear fruit, the regular calls did offer a valuable forum for the exchange of information and ideas. The authors coordinated and participated in all of these telephone conference calls.

15. Virginia, Pennsylvania, Connecticut, South Carolina, Georgia, and Ohio had commissions or advisory groups.

16. Interview with Matt Warschauer, Chairperson, Connecticut Civil War Commemoration Committee, February 10, 2016.

17. A comprehensive presentation of events is not possible in this chapter. As of late 2016, however, the nine states surveyed maintained websites that provide some record of their Sesquicentennial activities. While they vary widely in the amount and timeliness of the information they contain, these websites represent the best way to get a snapshot of what was done. See the following: http://www.ohiocivilwar150.org/; http://sc150civilwar.palmettohistory.org/; http://pacivilwar150.com/; http://www.virginiacivilwar.org/; http://web.ccsu.edu/civilwar/?redirected; http://www.gacivilwar.org/; http://www.archives.state.al.us/BA/; http://history.idaho.gov/idaho-150; and http://northwesthistory.blogspot.com/2013/01/crowdsourcing-civil-war-history-in.html.

18. See http://www.virginiacivilwar.org/. In addition to its Signature Series of seven conferences, Virginia's commission sponsored a History Mobile exhibit that toured the state; a major exhibition that opened at the Virginia Historical Society before visiting seven other venues; a smaller panel version that visited twenty state-wide venues; a statewide document project that scanned original source materials related to the Civil War and emancipation; an online database allowing users to search a soldier's history across Virginia's battlefields; a tourism grant program; and a closing concert at the state capitol. The topics for the seven Signature Conferences included: *America on the Eve of the Civil War*; *Race, Slavery and the Civil War: the Tough Stuff of American History*; *Military Strategy in the American Civil War*; *Leadership and Generalship in the American Civil War*; *The American Civil War at Home*; *the American Civil War in a Global Context*; and *Causes Won and Lost: The End of the Civil War*.

19. The Heinz Center produced two books—*The Civil War in Pennsylvania: A Photographic History* and *The Civil War in Pennsylvania: The African American Experience* as well as a joint journal issue on the Civil War in Pennsylvania combining publications by the PHMC, the Historical Society of Pennsylvania, and the Heinz History Center.

20. Quoted from "Ohio Civil War 150: Interpretive Framework" http://www.ohio civilwar150.org/resources/interpretive-framework/, accessed on March 2, 2016.

21. See http://www.ohiocivilwar150.org/. Exhibitions included: The Colors of War: Ohio Civil War Flags; Ohio Volunteer Infantry: The First Thirteen; the Enemy within: Copperheads and the Knights of the Golden Circle; Women on the Frontlines; A House Divided: How Ohio Politics Shaped the Civil War; Fighting For Freedom: African Americans during the Civil War; the Irish in the Civil War; and Lincoln's Air Force. *Ohio Civil War 150* has also been credited with changing how Ohioans think about public commemoration and paving the way for an upcoming statewide celebration of Neil Armstrong's moonwalk in 2019. Interview with Jackie Barton, Chief Program Officer, Ohio History Connection, February 19, 2016.

22. While Connecticut's close proximity to Massachusetts might reasonably lead to the conclusion that it shared its neighbor's strong anti-slavery heritage, the Constitution State did not finally abolish slavery until 1848. Furthermore, it was a locus for Copperhead activity throughout the Civil War.

23. Manuel Roig-Franzia, "At Charleston's Secession Ball, Divided Opinions on the Spirit of S.C.," *Washington Post*, December 22, 2010. http://www.washingtonpost.com/wp-dyn/content/article/2010/12/21/AR2010122105341.html?sid=ST2010122201695, accessed on February 23, 2016.

24. Interview with Eric Emerson, director and state historic preservation officer, South Carolina Department of Archives and History, February 17, 2016.

25. The Atlanta History Center scored a major coup when the City of Atlanta decided in 2014 to relocate the Atlanta Cyclorama to the organization's campus, where it will undergo extensive restoration before being installed in a new, purpose-built facility by 2018.

26. E-mail in author's possession from Lorraine McConaghy, Public Historian Emeritus at the Museum of History and Industry, February 2, 2016, and interview

with Janet Gallimore, executive director, Idaho State Historical Society, February 25, 2016.The Idaho Historical Society did mount a major exhibition on Abraham Lincoln.

27. *Holding the High Ground: A National Park Service Plan for the Sesqui-centennial of the American Civil War*, 2008, 6. https://hst409509.files.wordpress.com/2011/01/holding-the-high-ground.pdf, accessed on March 3, 2016.

28. Absent the federal largesse available during the Centennial commemoration, much of the interpretive infrastructure for the nation's major Civil War battlefields still dates from the early 1960s. Substantial improvements to interpretation were made at Richmond's Tredegar Iron Works, Fort Scott, and Shiloh. New visitor centers at Gettysburg and Fort Sumter represented major accomplishments. These were the exception, not the rule. E-mail from Dwight Pitcaithley in author's possession, March 9, 2016.

29. Interview with Robert Sutton, former chief historian for the NPS, February 12, 2016.

30. Warschauer interview.

31. Interview with Jackie Barton, chief program officer, Ohio History Connection, February 19, 2016

32. Katharine Q. Seelye, "Celebrating Secession Without the Slaves," *The New York Times*, November 29, 2010. http://www.nytimes.com/2010/11/30/us/30confed.html, accessed on March 3, 2016.

33. Emerson interview.

34. The complete stories for these markers can be accessed at the Georgia Historical Society website. See http://georgiahistory.com/ghmi_marker_updated/march-to-the-sea-ebenezer-creek/ (Ebenezer Creek); http://georgiahistory.com/ghmi_marker_updated/african-american-soldiers-in-combat/ (African American soldiers in combat); http://georgiahistory.com/ghmi_marker_updated/civil-war-slave-con spiracy/ (Slave conspiracy); and http://georgiahistory.com/ghmi_marker_updated/general-cleburnes-proposal-to-arm-slaves/ (Cleburne proposal).

35. Charles Oliver, "Marker Ensures Black Soldiers' Role Remembered in History," *Dalton Daily Citizen*, October 7, 2010. http://www.daltondailycitizen.com/news/local_news/marker-ensures-black-soldiers-role-remembered-in-history/article_0b3f979c-0fbc-50d8–8fdb-b706c068e1c1.html, accessed on February 23, 2016.

36. Interview with W. Todd Groce, president & chief executive officer, Georgia Historical Society, February 3, 2016.

37. Megan Matteucci, "NAACP Objects to MLK Drive Location for Civil War Marker," *Atlanta Journal-Constitution*, April 6, 2011. http://www.ajc.com/news/news/local/naacp-objects-to-mlk-drive-location-for-civil-war-/nQsJr/, accessed on February 23, 2016. The text for the marker on the destruction of Atlanta can be accessed at http://georgiahistory.com/ghmi_marker_updated/the-burning-and-destruction-of-atlanta/.

38. Seelye, "Celebrating Secession Without the Slaves."

39. Cook, 142. Robertson's connection to Civil War commemoration began 1961, when the thirty-year-old junior professor at the University of Iowa was hired as executive director of the Civil War Centennial Commission. There he managed the Commission's day-to-day operations under the general direction of Allan Nevins.

40. See *Confederate Odyssey: The George W. Wray Jr. Civil War Collection at the Atlanta History Center* (2014). The 450-page volume, published by the University of Georgia Press, was written by Dr. Gordon Jones, Senior Military Curator of the Atlanta History Center, with photography by Jack Melton.

41. Interview with Dwight Pitcaithley, February 9, 2016.

42. Alan Blinder and Richard Fausset, "Confederate Flag Down, but Black South Carolinians See Bigger Fights," *The New York Times*, July 20, 2015. http://www.nytimes.com/2015/07/21/us/confederate-flag-down-but-south-carolina-blacks-see-bigger-fights.html?_r=0, accessed on March 8, 2016.

43. Emerson interview.

44. Sutton interview.

45. Alan Blinder, "Momentum to Remove Confederate Symbols Slows or Stops," *The New York Times*, March 13, 2016. http://www.nytimes.com/2016/03/14/us/momentum-to-remove-confederate-symbols-slows-or-stops.html?emc=eta1, accessed on March 24, 2016.

46. Blinder and Fausset, "Confederate Flag Down."

Figure 13.1.   People gather in front of the Mother Emanuel AME Church on June 20, 2015 to commemorate a tragedy. Photo by George McDaniel.

Chapter 13

Commemorating Tragedy at Mother Emanuel AME Church

George W. McDaniel

What will it take, ask Rick Beard and Bob Beatty, "to cause a sea change in attitudes toward the Civil War's causes and consequences?" We might just as well wonder what's at stake if we don't. George W. McDaniel's heartfelt paean to the commemorative labors of a community struck by tragedy suggests one possibility and, in doing so, reinforces Manzullo-Thomas's observation that "public memory is often formed in the crucible of religious emotion." The setting in this case is Charleston, South Carolina, where in 2015 twenty-one year old Dylan Roof entered the historic Emanuel African Methodist Episcopal Church and murdered nine people in hopes of igniting a race war. The shooting occurred at a time, as McDaniel tell us, when mass killings had seemed to become a fixture in American life. And yet, the Charleston shooting was more than just that. What transpired at the old church, itself a monument to the modern civil rights movement, rattled our notion that decades of commemorative work had somehow relegated the terrors of race hatred to memory. McDaniel's essay is a forceful reckoning with the "dark side," as he puts it, but its strength lies not only in its emotional power. We find here too, outlined in practical terms, a commemorative prescription for resisting hatred during an era wherein heritage professionals have taken on the unlikely role of first responders.

—ed.

A black Hyundai parked near a handsome, historic African American church in Charleston, South Carolina. The building dated to 1891 and its congregation to 1816. A young white man with a bowl haircut emerged nicely but informally dressed. He walked through the unlocked side door and into the ground floor parish hall where a Bible study was underway. Twelve people, including the pastor, welcomed him. Gathered around a table, they discussed the reading for the day, Mark 4:16, Jesus' parable about the sow-ing of seeds. Close to an hour of discussion and prayer amicably passed by. The young man then stood up, pulled out a Glock semiautomatic pistol, and gunned down nine of the twelve, reloading with at least four clips and firing seventy-seven bullets. Each one was .45 of an inch in diameter upon enter-ing the body and probably wider upon exiting. He hurled racial epithets and proclaimed he had to do this. Before leaving, he told one lady, Polly Shep-pard, that he had spared her so she could tell the story. When apprehended, he turned out to be not wild-eyed or crazy looking, but instead, the kind of average-looking young white man who may be seen in communities across the nation.

This is but one instance of the hateful killings recently seen in America and across the world. One thing these killers have in common is they are often seen by neighbors and friends as having been "normal." For some reason, these killers have persuaded themselves, or been persuaded, that there are people so different from themselves and their own kind that those people have become the "Other," no longer fellow human beings who deserve to live. Such mental persuasions are not new, for we have heard them for centuries: "Heretic, Commie, Nigger, Fag, Pig, Jew, Gook, Infidel"—the list could go on. Such debasement—and often in America it is grounded in race—is interwoven into the warp and weft of our history and offers teach-able moments, so that we can explore the fallacy, indeed the tragedy, of such biased and fearful thinking. We avoid such knowledge at our peril because, as writers have told us for centuries, to deny the existence of evil is hubris, and hubris inevitably leads to tragedy.

For that reason alone, commemorations by historical organizations are important. They help us all understand that the dark side is very much a part of our history. We are not exceptional. We are not innocent. Adam and Eve are part of us all, as is the snake. Commemorations then can offer opportuni-ties for conversations, programs, exhibits, and other means by which we can better inform one another of who we are, amidst our diversity, and thereby develop a deeper and a more nuanced and humane appreciation of our simi-larities and differences. Being different should not result in being stigmatized as the "Other."

The good news is that in response to these recent killings, people have felt called to commemorate on their own in order to express sentiments opposite to the killers'. They wish to tell us that the victims are not the "Other" but are instead our fellow brothers and sisters. They may communicate this by carrying signs, proclaiming "Je suis Charlie" or "I am AME." They choose words that express their pain and their sense of loss, as well as their hopes and prayers for a brighter world, one in which we may, as John Lennon said decades ago, "come together." As they express themselves, some may wish to be alone, others may gather with family or in groups, small or large. Still others may testify, meditate, or give voice through music. Time and time again, we also see how people choose to endow tangible things, purchased or homemade, with their spiritual beliefs, feeling that words alone are not enough. By all of these ways, people wish to tell us that no one is the "Other," and that we are all brothers and sisters in one human family.

These were the sentiments expressed by scores of flowers, note cards, banners, posters, teddy bears, crosses, rosary beads, candles, paintings, photographs, and more when I came to pay my respects at Mother Emanuel AME in Charleston on Friday and Saturday, following the murders on Wednesday by that man in the black Hyundai. These things exemplified that moment in time both for Charleston and our nation. It had not rained yet, and as a former director of a historic site and as a Vietnam Veteran who has visited the Vietnam Memorial since its dedication, I was concerned that when the summer storms came, as surely they would in June, they would spoil the signed banners and artifacts left in homage.

Upon returning home, I called my friend Elizabeth "Liz" Alston, a longtime member of Mother Emanuel and its historian, and a former member of Drayton Hall's Site Council. I asked if the church had plans for preserving the artifacts in front of the church. She explained that, as a historian, she was thinking the same way, but that the church was in the midst of grieving and was focused on conducting funerals, caring for the bereaved, and on any number of other things. She too was devastated but nonetheless suggested we meet.

I called museum and preservation professionals, academic and public historians as well as African American descendants of the historic Drayton Hall plantation who had grown up near Emanuel. Each responded positively, and just a week after the tragedy, a small group of us met with Liz in the ground floor room where the shootings had taken place.

It was discomforting to be in that same space, yet also uplifting. We saw the life of the church continue as members young and old came and went, comforted one another, and got ready for the Bible study that evening, the same class conducted a week earlier with the assassin present. We had our meeting, got the ball rolling for preserving artifacts, and since it had not rained, we brought a number of them into the church, including a large cross, and stored them in a side room.

While we were retrieving artifacts, a half dozen pastors gathered for a press conference in front of the church. Speaking forthrightly into the television cameras, the principal speaker, the Rev. Nelson Rivers, a local pastor and leader in the civil rights movement, explained in no uncertain terms that this was the time for "respect." Protest has its time, but not at this time. These families had experienced loss beyond our understanding. I heard him declare forcefully: "Malcolm X was about respect. Martin Luther King was about respect. The civil rights movement is about respect. And if you don't understand respect, then you don't belong here at this time." It was a challenge and an assurance for our future. The memorabilia surrounding him underscored his call. That night a thunderstorm struck, making our retrieval just in time.

The next week, our group met again, assessed progress, and retrieved more artifacts. Key to our preservation efforts was the Charleston Archives, Libraries and Museums Council (CALM), which members of our group had called into action. Together, they devised a well-organized process by which artifacts would be systematically photographed in situ and then retrieved from the outside for safekeeping. The Smithsonian's National Museum of African American History and Culture provided national input and helped contextualize our work.

Since church space was so limited and in demand, Liz Alston contacted her friend, Mayor Joe Riley, and he quickly responded by offering both staff support as well as temporary storage space in a nearby community center until a more permanent home could be found. Working with church staff, CALM and other volunteers retrieved artifacts from the front of the church in a systematic way throughout the coming months. Their criteria included leaving the perishables like flowers in place and preserving a representative sample of the artifacts, not everything, since time and space did not allow it. Over time, we saved a total of 6,000 artifacts. A moving company, Two Men and a Truck, volunteered to move the artifacts from the church to the community center, where they were secured in a climatized, locked room. CALM and their volunteers also helped Emanuel by processing and cataloguing hundreds of letters and packages, many with Bibles, notes, paintings, sculpture, teddy bears, or quilts enclosed. CALM also reached out to the archival supply company, Gaylord Archival, and they generously donated folders, boxes, and other supplies. The conservation storage company, Iron Mountain, offered secure storage space, which may well be accepted in the near future. What still remains on view are the fire hydrant and crepe myrtles in front of the church, now covered with hand-written messages and signatures and serving as perpetual commemorations.

Since our initiative had been spur of the moment, after several months, it was evident that we needed to develop a long-range plan. John Hildreth, vice president of the eastern region of the National Trust and a member of our group, volunteered to facilitate this effort. Key questions included as follows: What was our relationship to the church? How long were we to remain in existence? What were our responsibilities? What were the conservation and cataloguing needs for the artifacts, and how were they to be met? What were we to keep, discard, or give to survivors, victims' families, or other organizations? What types of facilities were needed for long-term storage, and what might be available? Who was going to lead and manage this process, and how would it be funded?

Working within the chain of command of the church and not as a separate entity was deemed essential, so we decided to become the Memorabilia Subcommittee of Emanuel's Archives and History Committee, of which Alston was chairman. We also decided that we would operate through the first year anniversary and then, with input from the church, reassess our future later. We also wanted to meet with the leadership of the church and its congregation, convey our condolences, explain what we were doing and why, and answer questions. The curators in our group pressed for decisions about the culling and disposition of artifacts, the proper storage and cataloguing of them, and providing for their professional curation and care. Such decisions rested with church leadership, especially the pastor, and due to other priorities and changes in pastors, delays developed.

In tandem with our preservation of the physical artifacts was a project that represented a now vital and new direction in historic preservation. Undertaken by Lowcountry Africana and the College of Charleston's Lowcountry Digital History Initiative and the Avery Research Center for African American History and Culture, it sought to document local and national responses in the digital media. This included photographs and video generously contributed by professional and lay photographers, news outlets, both local and national, and individuals on social media, such as Facebook and Instagram. Their work culminated in an online exhibition, *A Tribute to the Mother Emanuel Church*, and was premiered at Mother Emanuel in May 2016. In powerful ways, this graphic account conveyed the outpouring of grief, sympathy, and hope as well as the efforts to address racial injustice and violence in Charleston and across the nation. Especially compelling were images of the many prayer vigils, marches, and protests against symbols such as the Confederate flag and calls for its removal from the SC Capitol grounds. Declared the Rev. Dr. Betty Deas Clark, pastor of Emanuel when it premiered, "We see this online tribute as a healing and educational resource."

To commemorate the first anniversary of the mass shootings, Emanuel developed services, public programs, and marches for June 15–25, 2016, and in early May asked the Memorabilia Subcommittee to produce an exhibit, using the artifacts we had preserved. Time was short, funding uncertain, and the exhibit theme undetermined. In a meeting with the pastor, the committee learned that the theme for the entire commemoration was to be "Victory in the Valley," and so we used words from the twenty-third psalm in writing the titles and language of the exhibit panels. We agreed that the accent should be on "healing," not forgiveness, because a lot of people had not yet forgiven, and it would be presumptive on our part to expect anyone to do so. In contrast, "healing" is a long, ongoing process, not a final state, and it recognizes both the sickness and the health in all of us. It is something we all need.

The City of Charleston donated the first floor of a building across the street from Emanuel. Thanks to volunteered funds, the History Workshop, a local exhibit design firm, was hired and donated a lot of their time. For the exhibit itself, a church member suggested we showcase quilts from the more than 400 sent to the church from around the world, many with inscriptions expressing heartache, sympathy, and the desire for healing. In addition, church members wanted to see the artifacts, so an exhibit case was filled with a representative samples, not neatly displayed, but placed at random and on top of one another as they had been in front of the church. To give context to the exhibit, a condensed version of the "Online Tribute" was shown on a wide screen. Volunteer docents were recruited and scheduled. A private viewing was offered for the victims' families and the survivors.

Since healing was the theme, integral to the exhibit was a place for visitor interaction. In the middle of one room was a panel inviting visitors to reflect on the exhibit and on their own situation, and then to identify one thing they could do to help "heal" their community upon their return home. They were asked to write that down on a card and deposit it in a box, and then it was for them to carry through with their pledge. In this way, we hoped that visitors would honor the victims and survivors not only by visiting the exhibit and participating in the commemoration programs but also by going back and doing something to help heal their own community and themselves. We hoped to turn museum experience into action.

This commemorative exhibit deeply touched visitors. It recognized the tragedy of the murders, the uplift of the responses, the challenges that lay ahead, and the hope to overcome them. Some of the most beautiful quilts represented the international response to the tragedy. Soon after the massacre, the Charleston Modern Quilt Guild had asked guilds across the world to send 4" x 6" blocks of cloth and to write inscriptions on them. Expecting a response of several hundred, the Guild received thousands from every state in the nation and nineteen countries overseas. They stitched the blocks into a multicolored composite, making a total of six quilts, two of which were exhibited. Upon each block were written brief prayers or words of comfort and the place of origin, which ranged from Australia and Oregon to Scotland and Switzerland. Even Mayor Joe Riley of Charleston submitted one. Inspired by President Obama's eulogy in Charleston, a member lovingly stitched in cursive the first verse of "Amazing Grace" across and down each quilt.

Attracting attention in one room was a large handsome white cloth with "A Love Letter from Dallas to Charleston" handwritten across the top, and in the center was a heart-shaped design filled with flowers, a gift from the Union

Coffee Shop, an outreach program of the Methodist Church in Dallas. On it, people had written prayers in differently colored inks, signed their names, and drawn crosses, flowers, faces, and more. Below the heart-shaped design was a large red stain. An arrow was drawn to it, accompanied by a note from the Rev. Mike Baughman, community curator of Union, which says:

> *We celebrated Communion on this banner. Some of the blood spilled. Christ is present, connecting our communities. I don't know you. You don't know me. We both know Jesus and that gives me hope.*

Draping the windows were 1,001 handcrafted origami cranes from a "Japanese Christian" church in California, with a letter explaining that cranes symbolized wishes for good fortune and hope for a better world in Japanese culture and that 1,000 means an abundance, so 1,001 means an abundance of abundances. In the exhibit case, visitors saw teddy bears, wooden crosses, rosary beads, a smooth pebble painted with the word "love," a Boston Marathon medal from the year after the bombing, and much more.

These responses, and others like them, made this commemoration worthwhile. Visitors, including survivors and relatives of victims, were deeply moved. For example, the sister of Myra Thompson, a victim, was so inspired that she wished to communicate with her deceased sister and left this note at the exhibit:

> *Dear Myra,*
>   *Today I experienced the most beautiful display of kind acts, love and deepest appreciation for you and my other brothers and sisters in Christ. All sorts of Art work were hung in your reverence.*

In the interactive exhibit, visitors placed eighty-seven note cards in the box, expressing their pledges to help heal. Some were general, such as a pledge to "be kind to everyone because we don't know the battles everyone is facing," or "initiate random acts of kindness whenever I see an opportunity." Some were specific and personal: "Spend more time and thought with my son who suffered from addiction and divorce"; "donate children's books to the library in memory of Cynthia Graham Hurd," a victim and a beloved librarian; "take every opportunity to add others to my circle of family and friends"; or "I walk past the church every day on my way to work. I will stop and pray every day for y'all." Others dealt more with public action, pledging to "confront and dismantle white privilege and institutional racism," or declaring "In my community, there was an act of violence toward a Muslim woman. I will advocate on her behalf and for religious tolerance." These were private and personal responses, with no monitoring, or follow-up by us, but from conversations with several who submitted cards, the invitation touched a chord.

At the end of June, the commemorative exhibit came down, but a number of visitors suggested that it become a traveling exhibit not just to mark the commemoration of the Emanuel tragedy but to generate ongoing efforts to help heal the brokenness of our communities. The Memorabilia Subcommittee supports this idea, and with the arrival of a new pastor at Mother Emanuel, decisions might be made soon. That more and more communities need help healing is tragically evident in the scourge of violence on view since the Mother Emanuel incident. On June 12, 2016, another hate-filled man murdered dozens at the Pulse nightclub in Orlando, Florida. In early July, two black men were killed by police officers, one in Baton Rouge, Louisiana, the other near St. Paul, Minnesota, and then an enraged black sniper shot and killed five police officers in Dallas, Texas, in retaliation. In Istanbul, Turkey, a trio of killers went on a rampage in the airport, while on Bastille Day, a man used a truck to mow down eighty or more innocent celebrants in Nice, France. The list could go on, each incident underscoring the fact that what I have described is not unique to Charleston. The man in the Hyundai takes many forms.

As such tragedies occur, historical organizations will be called upon to respond. While we in Charleston followed our hearts and responded on the spur of the moment, if we had to do it again, we would have initiated long-range planning much earlier. In fact, it would be wise for a local, state, or national professional association to begin now to put preliminary plans in place, which could serve as a template to be tailored to specific communities. Questions to be asked as soon as possible include the following:

- What is the mission of your organization, and how does responding to tragedy fit into it?
- What are the partnerships that might be formed?
- What is the chain of command?
- What are possible sources of funding?
- What collection policies best suit different types of memorabilia (e.g., artifacts, photographs, documents, and digital media), and where might these items be stored?
- What is the nature of the place where the tragedy occurred? Is it an open public space, a public building, a private building? Who is in charge of that place and of what happens to it? Who owns the artifacts left there?
- What are the capacities of staff and/or volunteers in light of their other priorities?
- What are the goals of commemoration, for project personnel and for various audiences?
- How does commemoration connect back to the victims' families, survivors, and their families and friends?

- How can commemoration provide teachable moments that help communities to heal and, ideally, prevent more tragedy?
- What can we do to prevent people from stigmatizing the "Other"?

All of us were surprised by what that young man in the black Hyundai did at Emanuel AME that June evening. But the hatred and the fear that consumed him are not new and should not surprise us. Looking to the future and to ensure that we do not forget, it is our responsibility to respond to such occurrences, preserve their history, develop honest commemorations, and seriously engage the public in them. We should strive to use the tragedy and the commemoration as teachable moments, moments that help heal both our minds and our hearts, so that chances for such tragedies to occur again are at least minimized and, we hope and pray, eliminated.

Figure 14.1.   Toni Morrison's "A Bench by the Road," Sullivan's Island, South Carolina.
Photo by Ron Cogswell.

Chapter 14

Afterword

Commemoration, Conversation, and Public Feeling in America Today

Erika Doss

The range of settings in which commemoration takes place, as we have seen throughout this volume, is matched only by the depth of emotion that runs through all facets of memory work. Certainly McDaniel's portrayal of the events in Charleston drives home the importance of allowing space in public memory for both the noble and the tragic. Painful though it may be, commemorating difficult pasts, as Erika Doss puts it, "broadens the scope and subjects of the national narrative." Indeed, none more than Doss have explored the significance of emotion in American commemorative life, which explains why her work and her ideas appear throughout the preceding essays. For Doss, then, we reserve the last word, an urging for all of us to reexamine our commemorative assumptions, particularly in conversation with the growing segments of today's audiences for whom moral accountability is neither objectionable nor optional.

—ed.

Commemoration, as Seth Bruggeman remarks in this book's introductory essay, "begins and ends in conversation with the many publics it might potentially serve."[1] Commemoration, in other words, is typically discursive—a kind of conversation, an act of speech or performance, a form of communication—that occurs when publics come together to remember, to honor, to celebrate, and/or to mourn people or events deemed significant, or exceptional, at particular moments. As a discursive cultural practice, commemoration can generate meaningful public conversations and spark the creative reexamination of conventional assumptions, acting in some cases as a catalyst for social and political change. In the United States in recent decades, the discursive terms of commemoration have been exceptionally fraught, an indication of increasingly factionalized conditions in contemporary American public culture and, in particular, angry disagreements about citizenship, belonging, identity, and democracy—the keywords framing the national narrative.

Despite these heated debates—or, most likely, because of them—commemoration is flourishing in America today. Memorials, festivals, pageants, fairs, museum exhibitions, battlefield reenactments, rituals, parades, and anniversary celebrations are organized and enacted every day in the United States, suggesting widespread local and national preoccupation with issues of memory and history accompanied by urgent desires to express—and claim—those concerns in visibly public contexts.[2] Identifying the "symbolic capital" inherent in commemoration, from the power it has to shape civic ideas and attitudes to the authority it asserts on social and political grounds, more and more Americans are claiming their rights to public memory.[3] The question or "conundrum" facing commemoration, Bruggeman poses, is how to make sense of the diverse and often competing public memories that it often embodies. Answers can be found, I suggest, in recognizing the role that feelings play in developing and directing public memory, and producing various forms of commemoration.

Commemoration is a highly emotional cultural practice, driven by the different kinds of feelings—gratitude, grief, shame, fear, anger, and hope, for example—that publics often have about the subjects they choose to remember. Increasing numbers of temporary memorials, for example, including spontaneous offerings and makeshift shrines erected at the sites of car accidents and school shootings, indicate how public feelings of grief and mourning are visibly expressed, and socially sanctioned, in America today. Scores of new war memorials, including the National World War II Memorial, dedicated in Washington, D.C., in 2004, represent abiding contemporary feelings of indebtedness and gratitude to the nation's military personnel and military endeavors. A growing body of shame-based memorials, in contrast, including the Salem Witchcraft Victims Memorial in Danvers, Massachusetts (dedicated in 1992), and the Proctor's Ledge Memorial in Salem (forthcoming, 2017), commemorate the mostly female victims of a pathological public culture of superstition and religious intolerance in the late seventeenth century, thereby challenge standard accounts of a heroic or triumphant national narrative. Other commemorative "sites of shame" address the subjects of slavery and lynching, raising questions about how to remember, represent, and perhaps redeem the nation's shameful histories of racial violence and intolerance.

Public feelings of anger also play a large role in contemporary commemorative practices: efforts in New Mexico and Texas in the late 1990s and early 2000s to pay tribute to Spanish conquistador Juan de Oñate, the leader of a colonizing expedition in 1598 who established the first European settlement in what became the United States while brutally suppressing the region's Indigenous inhabitants, were extraordinarily contentious.[4] Feelings of anger, in fact, are omnipresent in America today. Contrary to German philosopher

Jürgen Habermas's vision of an ideal public sphere in which sensible citizens invested in democratic intentions share ideas and debate issues, contemporary American public life is often marked by all-consuming emotional appeals and affective conditions that overpower, or diminish, efficacious and productive democratic goals.[5] Public feelings—and media narratives about these feelings—have been mobilized and manipulated in recent elections in America, and in current debates over health care, reproductive rights, immigration, and the "war on terror." Importantly, these amplified affective conditions do not foreclose social and political possibilities, including the transformative possibilities of democratic social change and political reform. But they do beg, as literary critic Lauren Berlant argues, for a "critical realm of the senses," a pedagogy of public feelings that considers how and why and which feelings shape historical moments, define concepts of citizenship, and relay ideas about self and national identity.[6] Recognizing the diverse public feelings embodied in various forms of commemoration helps us understand their competing public memories and cultural meanings, and imagine more efficacious possibilities for remembering in America today.

Consider, for example, the emotional tenor of the Bench by the Road Project, launched in February 18, 2006, on the occasion of American writer and Nobel laureate Toni Morrison's seventy-fifth birthday. In 1989, lamenting slavery's commemorative neglect in America and explaining why she wrote the novel *Beloved*, Morrison observed:

> There is no place you or I can go, to think about or not think about,
> to summon the presences of, or recollect the absences of slaves . . .
> There is no suitable memorial, or plaque, or wreath, or wall, or park,
> or skyscraper lobby. There's no 300-foot tower, there's no small
> bench by the road.

In July 2008, the Toni Morrison Society dedicated its first Bench by the Road memorial at Fort Moultrie on Sullivan's Island, South Carolina, near the point of entry into North America for about 40 percent of the millions of Africans who were enslaved in the country.[7] Maintained by the NPS, the memorial consists of a six-foot metal bench that faces the Intracoastal Waterway. A nearby plaque, mounted in a cement foundation on the ground next to the bench, reads: "Nearly half of all African Americans have ancestors who passed through Sullivan's Island."

In 2009, a second bench was dedicated in Oberlin, Ohio, a major center of nineteenth-century abolitionism and a destination for slaves fleeing the south. Its plaque states:

> This bench is placed in memory of the enslaved men, women and children
> who followed the path of the Underground Railroad and sought refuge in the

community of Oberlin, Ohio, in their quests for emancipation. Their spirit endures and will inspire us until every human is raised up to freedom.

To date, more than twenty Bench by the Road memorials have been erected in the United States and Europe: in Hattiesburg, Mississippi (2009, in honor of the Freedom Riders), Paris, France (2010, in memory of Louis Delgres, a black military officer who led the resistance against the reinstatement of slavery under Napoleon in the early nineteenth century), Mitchelville, South Carolina (2013, commemorating the nation's first self-governing community of freed slaves), Nyack, New York (2015, honoring Cynthia Hesdra, a former slave who became a "conductor" on the Underground Railroad and then a successful business woman and landowner), and Baton Rouge, Louisiana (2016, paying tribute to the city's 1953 bus boycott, an important act of dissent in the civil rights movement). Future benches are envisioned in other places of special significance in African American history or in Morrison's novels, including the site in Money, Mississippi where fourteen-year-old Emmett Till was murdered in 1955. The Toni Morrison Society encourages "corporations, community organizations, families, and individuals" to sponsor the commemorative benches, and provides information on costs ($3,500–$5,000, depending on bench size) and an online application form on its website.[8]

Commemorating "sites of shame" like Sullivan's Island, South Carolina or Money, Mississippi as significant sites of American history and memory broadens the scope and subjects of the national narrative. The cliché that history belongs to the winners does not apply when a nation's commemorative discourse is informed by its history of slavery, lynching, and racial profiling. Commemorations that acknowledge victims in the national narrative, thereby serve to critique the nation's imperfections, are increasing in America today, because Americans like Toni Morrison and millions of others want those public histories visibly remembered—and are not intimidated by how they challenge heroic or triumphant accounts of American history. Rather than adhering to shallow, or one-dimensional, stories of national progress, these histories admit the complications, contradictions, and obligations of American national identity. Doing so often involves reckoning with the nation's ghosts, with the specters from the past who continue to haunt the national imaginary.

The story of the development and commemoration of the African Burial Ground National Monument, located in Lower Manhattan and dedicated in 2007, is a prime example. The small "pocket-park" site (about one-third of an acre) includes an outdoor memorial and an indoor Visitor Center. Both commemorate the once much larger grounds (6.6 acres) where an estimated 20,000 enslaved Africans were interred from the late seventeenth century until the 1790s. As New York expanded in the nineteenth century, sacred space in what had been the city's outskirts became prime office space in downtown Manhattan, and the burial ground was filled in, paved over, and reconstituted with courthouses, department stores, theaters, and other buildings. The labor and lives of New York's formerly substantial slave population—in the mid-seventeenth century, 25 percent of Manhattan's Dutch colony comprised enslaved Africans; in 1737, 20 percent of the city's residents were slaves— were largely forgotten.[9]

In 1991, during the preconstruction survey for a $276 million, 34-story federal office building at 290 Broadway, just north of City Hall, archae-ologists discovered the human remains of more than 400 African slaves, many ritually interred in hexagonal wooden coffins pointing east, and some accompanied by symbolic funerary artifacts including coins, cowrie shells, buttons, beads, and pieces of coral. One coffin lid featured a heart-shaped design made of ninety-three iron nails, interpreted as either the West African symbol "Sankofa" (meaning "going backward to go forward") or "Akoma" (translated as patience and tolerance). The General Services Administration (GSA), the federal agency charged with overseeing government projects like office buildings, deemed the discovery significant but was lax in follow-ing archaeological and preservation standards, such that some of the burial findings were destroyed. African American historians, citizen activists, and politicians were incensed, and New York Mayor David Dinkins demanded that the GSA halt the excavation and adhere to specific federal mandates regarding the recovery and preservation of human remains. Recognizing the site's historic and public value, Congress designated it a National Historic Landmark in 1993 and mandated that the new federal office building feature "a world-class memorial museum and research center of African-American history and culture," including public artwork in its first-floor lobby and a permanent outdoor memorial. Also mandated was a ceremonial reburial of the site's human remains.[10] In October 2003, elaborate Rites of Ancestral Return was held, during which human remains and burial artifacts were reinterred at the site in seven specially designed wooden crypts. Writer Maya Angelou addressed a large crowd, remarking: "You may bury me in the bot-tom of Manhattan. I will rise. My people will get me. I will rise out of the huts of history's shame."[11]

Four years later, in a ceremony attended by thousands of people, the Afri-can Burial Ground National Monument was officially dedicated. Featuring an "Ancestral Chamber," a narrow, twenty-five foot tall and highly polished granite room intimating both the interior of a slave fort and a slave ship, the monument also includes an "Ancestral Libation Court," a sunken space, about four-feet below street level, embellished with symbols referencing the African Diaspora. The court's stone floor depicts a map of the world, with

West Africa at its center, and a small hole where libations are offered during ceremonies. Words engraved on the floor cite the thousands of slaves buried below: "Burial 205 woman between eighteen and twenty years" and "Burial 75 newborn or stillborn baby." Designed by architect Rodney Léon, the $5 million monument includes a "Memorial Wall" illustrating the physical boundaries of the original burial ground, and an "Ancestral Re-Interment Grove" marked by seven grassy mounds and a grove of trees. A "Wall of Remembrance" facing the street bordering the memorial reads: "For all those who were lost, For all those who were stolen, For all those who were left behind, For all those who were not forgotten."

On this tiny plot of land—less than a fraction of the acreage occupied by the National September 11 Memorial and Museum at the World Trade Center, located a few blocks south—slavery's shameful history in New York is visibly confronted and commemorated. That history is acknowledged in terms that downplay victimization and that appeal, especially, to the ethics of work. Rather than explicitly referencing the pain and trauma of human bondage, or rendering that bondage on heroic terms, the African Burial Ground National Monument reminds visitors of the tens of thousands of enslaved Africans who built the City of New York and enabled its enormous colonial, and eventually national, profits.

Work, and notions of a moralizing work ethic, have long been central to American understandings of self and national identity; as Frederick Douglass remarked in 1853, "Men are not valued in this country, or in any country, for what they *are*; they are valued for what they do."[12] Work, a value and a sentiment that has repeatedly granted legitimacy and enabled citizenship in the national narrative, is employed in this memorial to shame visitors about slavery's erasure in American history: indeed, the shame of slavery as related here is the shame of forgetting slavery's *labor* in the making of the nation. In a memorial that is simultaneously a cemetery and a ceremonial center, America's haunted legacy of slavery is revealed and remembered, and the scope of national subjectivity is expanded, via the inclusionary terms of labor.

In 2006, when the African Burial Ground was designated a National Monument, Department of Interior Secretary Gale Norton remarked: "After facing this painful past, we come together to preserve this sacred ground. This burial ground teaches slavery's shame. It also teaches that repentance and remembrance lead to renewal."[13] As Aaron Lazare argues, the accountability of American national identity includes both pride and shame:

> People are not guilty for actions in which they did not participate. But just as people take pride in things for which they had no responsibility (such as famous ancestors . . . and great accomplishments of their nation), so, too must these people accept

the shame . . . of their family . . . and their nations. Accepting national pride must include willingness to accept national shame when one's country has not measured up . . . this accountability is what we mean when we speak of having a national identity.[14]

Indeed, one explanation for shame's surfacing in American commemoration today is heightened attention to issues of moral accountability: to recognize, for example, the dual terms of slavery *and* freedom in the shape and direction of the national narrative. Expectations that nations, for example, "act morally and acknowledge their own gross historical injustices" emerge from shared public feelings that they have failed to live up to their ideals and can, often through commemorative acts, work to right those wrongs. Commemorating "sites of shame" can, then, serve as a revitalizing instrument of shared national purpose attuned to redeeming the past.[15] Like other public feelings, shame has enormous affective possibilities and can be emotionally productive in shaping and directing the discursive terms of today's commemorative practices.

NOTES

1. Seth C. Bruggeman, "Introduction: Conundrum and Nuance in American Memory," in Seth C. Bruggeman, ed. *Commemoration: The American Association of State and Local History Guide* (Lanham, MD: Rowman & Littlefield, 2017), 13.

2. Erika Doss, *Memorial Mania: Public Feeling in America* (Chicago, IL: University of Chicago Press, 2010).

3. On "symbolic capital," see Pierre Bourdieu, *Outline of a Theory of Practice* (Cambridge: Cambridge University Press, 1977), 114–120.

4. Erika Doss, "Who Owns Historical Memory? Commemorative Conflicts in the American Southwest," in Tomasz Basiuk, Sylwia Kuzma-Markowska, and Krystyna Mazur, eds. *The American Uses of History: Essays on Public Memory* (Frankfurt am Main: Peter Lang, 2011), 17–30.

5. Jürgen Habermas, *The Structural Transformation of the Public Sphere: An Inquiry into a Category of Bourgeois Society*, trans. Thomas Burger (1962; Cambridge: MIT Press, 1989).

6. Lauren Berlant, "Critical Inquiry, Affirmative Culture," *Critical Inquiry* 30 (Winter 2004), 446.

7. Toni Morrison, "A Bench by the Road," *The World Journal of the Unitarian Universalist Association* 3, no. 1 (January/February 1989), 4; Felicia R. Lee, "Bench of Memory at Slavery's Gateway," *New York Times* (28 July 2008), E-1.

8. See "Bench By the Road Project," at the official website of the Toni Morrison Society. http://www.tonimorrisonsociety.org/bench.html.

9. See Michele Bogart, "Public Space and Public Memory in New York's City Hall Park," *Journal of Urban History* 25, no. 2 (1999), 226–257; and Sarah R. Katz,

"Redesigning Civic Memory: The African American Burial Ground in Lower Manhattan" (PhD dissertation, University of Pennsylvania, 2006); on slave population statistics see Christopher Moore, "A World of Possibilities: Slavery and Freedom in Dutch New Amsterdam" and Jill Lepore, "The Tightening Vise: Slavery and Freedom in British New York," both included in Ira Berlin and Leslie M. Harris, eds. *Slavery in New York* (New York: New Press, 2005), 38 and 60, respectively.

10. Katz, *Redesigning Civic Memory*, 59–60.

11. Katz, *Redesigning Civic Memory*, 87.

12. Frederick Douglass, "Free Blacks Must Learn Trades," in *Frederick Douglass: The Narrative and Selected Writings*, ed. Michael Meyer (New York: Modern Library, 1984), 350.

13. "Secretary Norton Announces President's Designation of African Burial Ground as a National Monument," *News Release, Department of the Interior* (February 28, 2006), at http://www.doi.gov/news/06_News_Releases/060228.htm.

14. Aaron Lazare, *On Apology* (New York: Oxford University Press, 2004), 41.

15. Elazar Barkan, *The Guilt of Nations: Restitution and Negotiating Historical Injustices* (Baltimore, MD: The John Hopkins University Press, 2000), xvi; see also Robert Drinan, *The Mobilization of Shame: A World View of Human Rights* (New Haven: Yale University Press, 2002).

Bibliography

Adair, Bill, Benjamin Filene, and Laura Koloski, eds. *Letting Go? Sharing Authority in a User-Generated World.* Philadelphia: The Pew Center for Arts and Heritage, 2011.

Anderson, Benedict. *Imagined Communities: Reflections on the Origin and Spread of Nationalism.* New York and London: Verso, 1983.

Anderson, Jay. *Time Machines: The World of Living History.* Nashville, TN: American Association for State and Local History, 1984.

Assmann, Aleida and Sebastian Conrad, eds. *Memory in a Global Age: Discourses, Practices, and Trajectories.* Basingstoke: Palgrave Macmillan, 2010.

Barthel, Diane L. *Historic Preservation: Collective Memory and Historical Identity.* New Brunswick, NJ: Rutgers University Press, 1996.

Blight, David W. *Race and Reunion: The Civil War in American Memory.* Cambridge, MA: Harvard University Press, 2001.

Bodnar, John. *The "Good War" in American Memory.* Baltimore, MD: Johns Hopkins University Press, 2011.

Bodnar, John. *Remaking America: Public Memory, Commemoration, and Patriotism in the Twentieth Century.* Princeton, NJ: Princeton University Press, 1993.

Bruggeman, Seth C., ed. *Born in the U.S.A.: Birth, Commemoration, and Public Memory.* Amherst: University of Massachusetts Press, 2012.

Bruggeman, Seth C. *Here, George Washington Was Born: Memory, Material Culture, and the Public History of a National Monument.* Athens: University of Georgia Press, 2008.

Chambers, Thomas A. *Memories of War: Visiting Battlegrounds and Bonefields in the Early American Republic.* Ithaca, NY: Cornell University Press, 2012.

Chiang, Min-Chin. *Memory Contested, Locality Transformed: Representing Japanese Colonial 'Heritage' in Taiwan.* Leiden: Leiden University Press, 2012.

Cook, Robert. *Troubled Commemoration: The American Civil War Centennial, 1961–1965.* Baton Rouge: Louisiana State University Press, 2007.

Cooper, Karen Coody. *Spirited Encounters: American Indians Protest Museum Poli-cies and Practices*. Lanham, MD: Alta Mira Press, 2008.

De Cesari, Chiara and Ann Rigney, eds. *Transnational Memory: Circulation, Articu-lation, Scales*. Berlin: Walter De Gruyter, 2014.

Dickey, Jennifer W. *A Tough Little Patch of History: Gone with the Wind and the Politics of Memory*. Fayetteville: University of Arkansas Press, 2014.

Doss, Erika. *Memorial Mania: Public Feeling in America*. Chicago, IL: University of Chicago Press, 2010.

Dubin, Steven. *Displays of Power: Controversy in the American Museum from the Enola Gay to Sensation*. New York and London: New York University Press, 1999.

Ferentinos, Susan. *Interpreting LGBT History at Museums and Historic Sites*. Lan-ham, MD: Rowman & Littlefield Publishers, 2014.

Flake, Kathleen. "Re-placing Memory: Latter-day Saints Use of Historical Monu-ments and Narrative in the Early Twentieth Century." *Religion an American Cul-ture: A Journal of Interpretation* 13, no. 1 (2003), 69–109

Frisch, Michael. *A Shared Authority: Essays on the Craft and Meaning of Oral and Public History*. Albany: State University of New York Press, 1990.

Gallagher, Gary. *Lee and His Generals in War and Memory*. Baton Rouge: Louisiana State University Press, 1998.

Gessner, Ingrid. "The Aesthetics of Commemorating 9/11: Towards A Transnational Typology of Memorials." *Journal of Transnational American Studies* 1, no. 6 (2015). http://escholarship.org/uc/item/7pw6k038.

Gillis, John R. *Commemorations: The Politics of National Identity*. Princeton, NJ: Princeton University Press, 1996.

Glassberg, David. *American Historical Pageantry: The Uses of Tradition in the Early Twentieth Century*. Chapel Hill: University of North Carolina Press, 1990.

Gobel, David and Daves Rossell, eds. *Commemoration in America: Essays on Monu-ments, Memorialization, and Memory*. Charlottesville and London: University of Virginia Press, 2013.

Gordon, Tammy S. *Private History in Public: Exhibition and the Settings of Everyday Life*. Lanham, MD: AltaMira, 2010.

Gordon, Tammy S. *The Spirit of 1976: Commerce, Community, and the Politics of Commemoration*. Amherst: University of Massachusetts Press, 2013.

Halbwachs, Maurice. *On Collective Memory*, ed. and trans. by Lewis A. Coser. Chi-cago, IL: University of Chicago Press, 1992.

Handler, Richard and Eric Gable. *The New History in an Old Museum: Creating the Past at Colonial Williamsburg*. Durham, NC: Duke University Press, 1997.

Hartje, Robert G. *Bicentennial USA: Pathways to Celebration*. Nashville, TN: The American Association for State and Local History, 1973.

Harwitt, Martin. *An Exhibit Denied: Lobbying and the History of the Enola Gay*. New York: Copernicus, 1996.

Hebel, Udo J., ed. *Transnational American Memories*. Berlin: Walter de Gruyter, 2009.

Heideking, Jurgen, Genevieve Fabre, and Kai Dreisbach, eds. *Celebrating Ethnicity and Nation: American Festive Culture from the Revolution to the Early 20th Cen-tury*. New York: Berghahn Books, 2001.

Horton, James Oliver, and Lois E. Horton. *Slavery and Public History: The Tough Stuff of American Memory.* Chapel Hill: University of North Carolina Press, 2008.

Jakle, John A., and Keith A. Sculle. *Remembering Roadside America: Preserving the Recent Past as Landscape and Place.* Knoxville: University of Tennessee Press, 2011.

Kammen, Carol. *On Doing Local History.* 2nd ed. Lanham, MD: AltaMira Press, 2003.

Kammen, Michael. *Mystic Chords of Memory: The Transformation of Tradition in American Culture.* New York: Vintage Books, 1991.

Kelman, Ari. *A Misplaced Massacre: Struggling Over the Memory of Sand Creek.* Cambridge, MA: Harvard University Press, 2013.

Kirshenblatt-Gimblett, Barbara. *Destination Culture: Tourism, Museums, and Heritage.* Berkeley: University of California Press, 1998.

Kössler, Reinhart. "Entangled History and Politics: Negotiating the Past Between Namibia and Germany." *Journal of Contemporary African Studies* 26 (July 2008), 313–339.

Kurashige, Lon. *Japanese American Celebration and Conflict: A History of Ethnic Identity and Festival, 1934–1990.* Berkeley: University of California Press, 2002.

Landsberg, Alison. *Prosthetic Memory: The Transformation of American Remembrance in the Age of Mass Culture.* New York: Columbia University Press, 2004.

Lepore, Jill. *The Whites of Their Eyes: The Tea Party's Revolution and the Battle over American History.* Princeton, NJ; and Oxford: Princeton University Press, 2010.

Levin, Amy K., ed. *Defining Memory: Local Museums and the Construction of History in America's Changing Communities.* Lanham, MD: AltaMira, 2007.

Levy, Daniel Levy and Natan Sznaider. *The Holocaust and Memory in the Global Age.* Philadelphia, PA: Temple University Press, 2006.

Linenthal, Edward T. *Preserving Memory: The Struggle to Create America's Holocaust Museum.* New York: Columbia University Press, 2001.

Linenthal, Edward T. *Sacred Ground: Americans and Their Battlefields.* Champaign: University of Illinois Press, 1993.

Linenthal, Edward T. and Tom Engelhardt. *History Wars: The* Enola Gay *and Other Battles for the American Past.* New York: Holt and Company, 1996.

Lowenthal, David. *The Past is a Foreign Country.* New York: Cambridge University Press, 1985.

Lowenthal, David. *Possessed by the Past: The Heritage Crusade and the Spoils of History.* New York: Free Press, 1996.

Magelssen, Scott and Rhona Justice-Malloy, eds. *Enacting History.* Tuscaloosa: University Press of Alabama, 2011.

Marling, Karal Ann. *George Washington Slept Here: Colonial Revivals and American Culture, 1876–1986.* Cambridge, MA: Harvard University Press, 1988.

McDonnell, Michael A., Clare Corbould, Frances M. Clarke, and W. Fitzhugh Brundage, eds. *Remembering the Revolution: Memory, History, and Nation Making from Independence to the Civil War.* Amherst and Boston: University of Massachusetts Press, 2013.

Melber, Henning. "Namibia's Past in the Present: Colonial Genocide and Liberation Struggle in Commemorative Narratives." *South African Historical Journal* 54 (2005), 91–111.

Meskell, Lynn. *Global Heritage: A Reader*. London: Wiley-Blackwell, 2015.

Miyamoto, Yuki. *Beyond the Mushroom Cloud: Commemoration, Religion, and Responsibility After Hiroshima*. New York: Fordham University Press, 2012.

Nora, Pierre. "Between History and Memory: Les Lieux de Mémoire." *Representations* 26 (Spring 1989), 7–24.

Oldfield, J.R. *'Chords of Freedom': Commemoration, Ritual, and British Transatlantic Slavery*. Manchester: Manchester University Press, 2007.

Olson, Daron. *Vikings across the Atlantic: Emigration and the Building of a Greater Norway, 1860–1945*. Minneapolis: University of Minnesota Press, 2013.

Overland, Orm. *Immigrant Minds, American Identities: Making the United States Home, 1870–1930*. Urbana: University of Illinois Press, 2000.

Phillips, Kendall, and G. Mitchell Reyes. *Global Memoryscapes: Contesting Remembrance in a Transnational Age*. Tuscaloosa: The University of Alabama Press, 2011.

Pickles, Katie. *Transnational Outrage: The Death and Commemoration of Edith Cavell*. Basingstoke: Palgrave Macmillan, 2007.

Rothberg, Michael. *Multidirectional Memory: Remembering the Holocaust in the Age of Decolonization*. Stanford, CA: Stanford University Press, 2009.

Rozensweig, Roy and David Thelen. *The Presence of the Past: Popular Uses of History in American Life*. New York: Columbia University Press, 1998.

Russo, David J. *Keepers of Our Past: Local Historical Writing in the United States, 1820s–1930s*. New York: Greenwood Press, 1988.

Savage, Kirk. *Monument Wars: Washington, D.C., the National Mall, and the Transformation of the Memorial Landscape*. Berkeley: University of California Press, 2011.

Savage, Kirk. *Standing Soldiers, Kneeling Slaves: Race, War, and Monument in Nineteenth-Century America*. Princeton, NJ: Princeton University Press, 1997.

Schultz, April R. *Ethnicity on Parade: Inventing the Norwegian American through Celebration*. Amherst: University of Massachusetts Press, 1994.

Seeyle, John. *Memory's Nation: The Place of Plymouth Rock*. Chapel Hill: The University of North Carolina Press, 1998.

Stern, Steve J. *Reckoning with Pinochet: The Memory Question in Democratic Chile, 1989–2006*. Durham, NC: Duke University Press, 2010.

Sturken, Marita. *Tangled Memories: The Vietnam War, the AIDS Epidemic, and the Politics of Remembering*. Berkeley: University of California Press, 1997.

Sturken, Marita. *Tourists of History: Memory, Kitsch, and Consumerism from Oklahoma City to Ground Zero*. Durham, NC: Duke University Press, 2007.

Summerhill, Stephen J. and John Alexander Williams. *Sinking Columbus: Contested History, Cultural Politics, and Mythmaking during the Quincentenary*. Gainesville: University of Florida Press, 2000.

Thompson, Jenny. *War Games: Inside the World of 20th-Century War Reenactors*. Washington, DC: Smithsonian Books, 2010.

Turino, Kenneth C. and Susan Ferentinos. "Entering the Mainstream, Interpreting LGBT History." *History News* 67, no. 4 (Autumn 2012), 21–25.

Tyson, Amy. *The Wages of History: Emotional Labor on Public History's Front Lines*. Boston, MA; and Amherst, MA: University of Massachusetts Press, 2013.

Ulrich, Laurel Thatcher. *The Age of Homespun: Objects and Stories in the Creation of an American Myth*. New York: Alfred A. Knopf, 2001.

Waldstreicher, David. *In the Midst of Perpetual Fetes: The Making of American Nationalism, 1776–1820*. Chapel Hill: University of North Carolina Press, 1997.

Walker, William S. *A Living Exhibition: The Smithsonian and the Transformation of the Universal Museum*. Amherst: University of Massachusetts Press, 2013.

Wallace, Mike. *Mickey Mouse History and Other Essays on American Memory*. Philadelphia, PA: Temple University Press, 1996.

Wenger, Beth. *History Lessons: The Creation of American Jewish Heritage*. Princeton, NJ: Princeton University Press, 2010.

Williams, Paul. *Memorial Museums: The Global Rush to Commemorate Atrocities*. Oxford and New York: Berg, 2007.

Winter, Jay. *Remembering the War: The Great War between History and Memory in the Twentieth Century*. New Haven, CT: Yale University Press, 2006.

Witz, Leslie. *Apartheid's Festival: Contesting South Africa's National Pasts*. Bloomington: Indiana University Press, 2003.

Yoneyama, Lisa. "Battles Over Memory in 'Culture Wars': A Trans-Pacific Perspective." *Nanzan Review of American Studies* 32 (2010), 9–20.

Young, Alfred F. *The Shoemaker and the Tea Party: Memory and the American Revolution*. Boston, MA: Beacon Press, 2000.

Young, James E. *The Texture of Memory: Holocaust Memorials and Meaning*. New Haven, CT: Yale University Press, 1993.

Zelizer, Barbie. *Remembering to Forget: Holocaust Memory through the Camera's Eye*. Chicago, IL: The University of Chicago Press, 1998.

Index

About the Contributors

Rick Beard is an independent historian, writer, and exhibition consultant with several decades of experience as a content developer and administrator. He served as a senior adviser to Pennsylvania Civil War 150.

Bob Beatty is Chief of Engagement for the American Association for State and Local History, Since 2007, Bob has served AASLH as interim president and CEO, chief operating officer, and vice president for programs, leading AASLH's professional development program including workshops, an annual meeting, affinity groups and other initiatives, and publications as editor of History News and the AASLH Editorial Board. He is author of *Florida's Highwaymen: Legendary Landscapes* (Historical Society of Central Florida, 2005); coeditor of *Zen and the Art of Local History* (Rowman & Littlefield, 2014), and author of *An AASLH Guide to Making Public History* (forthcoming from Rowman & Littlefield).

Erika Doss is a professor in the Department of American Studies at the University of Notre Dame. Her publications include *Benton, Pollock, and the Politics of Modernism: From Regionalism to Abstract Expressionism* (1991, which received the Charles C. Eldredge Prize), *Spirit Poles and Flying Pigs: Public Art and Cultural Democracy in American Communities* (1995), *Elvis Culture: Fans, Faith, and Image* (1999), *Looking at Life Magazine* (editor, 2001), *Twentieth-Century American Art* (2002), *The Emotional Life of Contemporary Public Memorials: Towards a Theory of Temporary Memorials* (2008), and *Memorial Mania: Public Feeling in America* (2010). The recipient of several Fulbright awards, Doss has also held fellowships at the Stanford Humanities Center, the Georgia O'Keeffe Museum Research Center, and the Smithsonian American Art Museum.

Janet L. Gallimore is the executive director of the Idaho State Historical Society. A graduate of the J. Paul Getty Museum Management Institute, Ms. Gallimore is currently a member of the Board of the American Association of State and Local History and a member of the Steering Committee for the History Relevance Campaign.

Tammy S. Gordon is an associate professor in the History Department at North Carolina State University, where she teaches public history and modern U.S. history. Her research focuses on historical memory and the leisure economy in recent history, and she is the author of two books: *Private History in Public: Exhibition and the Settings of Everyday Life* (Alta Mira Press, 2010) and *The Spirit of 1976: Commerce, Community, and the Politics of Commemoration* (University of Massachusetts Press, 2013).

Patrick Grossi is director of advocacy at the Preservation Alliance for Greater Philadelphia. As a public historian and place-based advocate, he has previously worked with the Philadelphia History Museum at the Atwater Kent, Wyck Historic House & Garden, the Pennsylvania Horticultural Society, and Friends of the Rail Park. Prior to joining the Preservation Alliance, Grossi served as project manager of Temple Contemporary's *Funeral for a Home*.

Adam Hjorthén has a PhD in history from Stockholm University, where he is a postdoctoral research fellow at the Department of Culture and Aesthetics and the president of the Swedish Association for American Studies. He is the author of *Cross-Border Commemoration: Celebrating Swedish Settling in America* (forthcoming from the University of Massachusetts Press).

Devin Manzullo-Thomas is director of the Sider Institute for Anabaptist, Pietist and Wesleyan Studies at Messiah College (Grantham, Pennsylvania). He also serves as archives coordinator for the college's Ernest L. Boyer Center. Devin regularly teaches courses in the history, biblical and religious Studies, peace and conflict studies, and interdisciplinary studies departments at the College. His research concerns the history of the Brethren in Christ Church and the public history of American religion, including the ways in which religious communities construct, commemorate, and contest the past in public through historical societies, heritage sites, museums, monuments, archives, and other institutions of public memory.

George W. McDaniel, PhD, is president of McDaniel Consulting, LLC and is now executive director emeritus of Drayton Hall, after serving as its executive director for twenty-five years and spearheading its work in preservation and community outreach. Drawing from his experience with Emanuel AME and historical organizations, he is helping museums and community organizations to enhance cross-cultural understanding, to promote civic engagement, and strive for bridge-building.

Jean-Pierre Morin is staff historian for Canada's department of Aboriginal Affairs and Northern Development (AANDC). He specializes in the history of treaties between the government and aboriginal people and the history of government policy and administration of AANDC. In recent years, he has worked at developing new interactive digital historical learning tools, web content and digital media as well as leading ongoing national commemoration initiatives such as the bicentennial of the War of 1812 and the 250th anniversary of the Royal Proclamation of 1763.

Anne C. Reilly is the executive director of the Plymouth Antiquarian Society in Plymouth, Massachusetts. She received her PhD in the History of American Civilization from the University of Delaware. Her dissertation, "Birthplaces of a Nation: Public Commemorations of American Origins in the Early Twentieth Century," explores the creation of memorial landscapes for the 300th anniversaries of the Jamestown (1907), Plymouth (1920), and New Sweden (1938) colonies.

Cathy Stanton teaches anthropology at Tufts University in Medford, Massachusetts, and is an active public humanist. Her current work focuses on the histories of food and farming in New England; with Michelle Moon, she is coauthor of *Public History and the Food Movement: Adding the Missing Ingredient* (Routledge, 2017).

Kenneth C. Turino, manager of Community Engagement and Exhibitions at Historic New England, has taught for over twenty years in the Tufts University Museum Studies Program where he teaches a courses on exhibitions and the future of historic houses. Mr. Turino is on the American Association for State and Local History's Council and has written several articles on interpreting LGBTQ history.

William S. Walker is associate professor of history at the Cooperstown Graduate Program (SUNY Oneonta). He is the author of *A Living Exhibition: The Smithsonian and the Transformation of the Universal Museum* and colead editor of History@Work, the blog of the National Council on Public History.

About the Editor

Seth C. Bruggeman is an associate professor of history at Temple University, where he periodically directs the Center for Public History. His books include an edited volume, *Born in the USA: Birth and Commemoration in American Public Memory*, and *Here, George Washington Was Born: Memory, Material Culture, and the Public History of a National Monument*.